# DON'T BUY YOUR RETIREMENT HOME WITHOUT

# DON'T BUY YOUR RETIREMENT HOME WITHOUT Me!

*Avoid the traps and
get the best deal when
buying a home in a
retirement community*

## RICHARD ANDREWS

**Wrightbooks**

First published in 2012 by Wrightbooks
an imprint of John Wiley & Sons Australia, Ltd
42 McDougall St, Milton Qld 4064

Office also in Melbourne

Typeset in Bembo Regular 11.5/14

National Library of Australia Cataloguing-in-Publication data:

| Author: | Andrews, Richard. |
|---|---|
| Title: | Don't buy your retirement home without me!: avoid the traps and get the best deal when buying a home in a retirement community / Richard Andrews. |
| ISBN: | 9780730377702 (pbk.) |
| Subjects: | Retirees—Australia—Housing. |
| | Retirement—Australia—Planning. |
| | Retirement communities—Australia. |
| | Retirees—Australia—Economic conditions. |
| Dewey Number: | 363.59460994 |

Cover design by Peter Reardon, Pipeline Design <www.pipelinedesign.com.au>

Cover image: © DSGpro/iStockphoto.com

Printed in China by Printplus Limited

10 9 8 7 6 5 4 3 2 1

**Disclaimer**
The material in this publication is of the nature of general comment only, and neither purports nor intends to be advice. Readers should not act on the basis of any matter in this publication without considering (and if appropriate, taking) professional advice with due regard to their own particular circumstances. The author and publisher expressly disclaim all and any liability to any person, whether a purchaser of this publication or not, in respect of anything and of the consequences of anything done or omitted to be done by any such person in reliance, whether whole or partial, upon the whole or any part of the contents of this publication.

*This book is dedicated to my beautiful kindred spirit, Nicole.*
*You complete me.*

# Contents

## Part V: The purchase     135

## Part VI: Living and leaving     169

# About the author

Richard Andrews is a property investment professional who has spent much of his career in senior roles in the property funds management industry. In 2009, Richard started the company Find My Retirement Home to provide specialist advice and buyers agency services to retirees looking to purchase a retirement home. Richard also provides training and accreditation to professional advisers, such as accountants, solicitors and financial planners, so they can give advice to their own clients around retirement home transactions.

Richard is a graduate of the Royal Military College, Duntroon. He has a Bachelor of Business (Hotel Management) and a Graduate Diploma of Applied Finance and Investment.

# Introduction

Hi there! Thanks for purchasing *Don't Buy Your Retirement Home Without Me!*—the book that retirement village sales agents *don't* want you to see! It is full of insider information and tips to help you find the right retirement home and then negotiate the best deal possible.

It seems like everyone I meet these days has a horror story of a friend or relative being ripped off by a retirement village somewhere. This is mainly due to the complexity of retirement home purchase contracts, and the hidden fees and charges that create many traps for the unwary buyer. The retirement industry itself has moved from a largely not-for-profit operating base to a fully fledged property sector, now dominated by investment banks and property developers, who are keen to make a quick buck to be made from our ageing population. Never has the need been greater for quality, independent advice and information on buying a retirement home for some of the most vulnerable members of our society.

It was for this purpose that I founded Find My Retirement Home, a company that provides independent advice and buyers agency services to retirees looking to purchase a retirement home. My mission is to help you get the best deal possible on your retirement home purchase.

This book is part of my commitment to inform buyers about retirement home transactions. It is designed to guide you through the whole purchase process, from the decision to downsize out of your existing home to settling into your new retirement community.

But first, let me to tell you how this all came about...

## The Find My Retirement Home story

In 2008 I was working as investment manager for a boutique listed property fund manager performing mergers and acquisitions. One of the main projects I was tasked to deliver was a $400 million luxury retirement-living development fund that consisted of six development sites and one operating retirement village in Australia and New Zealand. We hoped to attract institutional investors, such as superannuation funds, to invest in the development and then own and operate the assets.

I had not worked in the retirement living sector before but had extensive experience in the hotel and commercial property sector working for institutional property owners. I thought my hotel accommodation background would be easily transferable to the retirement living sector — how wrong I was!

For nine months I led a team that researched the sector, analysed the properties and modelled the financial performance of the seven retirement villages and the fund itself. I was stunned by the complexities of the contract and financial arrangements that the purchasers of retirement homes were obliged to understand and sign off on. Village owners had clearly spent much time and money obtaining professional advice on how to structure these agreements to keep within the retirement villages' legislation regime while maximising their own profits. If it took my crack team nine months to figure it all out, how were people without our skills and training meant to do it?

As it turned out, we were unable to get the fund established before the global financial crisis hit the markets and institutions decided that their cash was better off in the bank than invested in risky property developments. Despite this setback, however, I now knew how retirement home purchase contracts worked and had become fascinated by the sector.

About a year later I had left the company and was working for myself, consulting to various organisations in the hotel and retirement property sectors. While doing research for a retirement village client, it struck me that there was no-one in the retirement sector giving impartial and independent advice or assistance to people wanting to buy a retirement home. Sure, there were lawyers around who could provide legal advice on the contracts, and financial planners who could probably tell you how much you could afford to spend, but there was no-one who could give retirement home buyers sound commercial and property advice about their purchase.

This led to the idea for starting my company Find My Retirement Home (my mum came up with the name—thanks Mum!), which was officially launched shortly thereafter.

Our mission is quite simply to help you get the best deal possible on your retirement home purchase.

We are the people's advocate and use our experience and negotiating skills to drive better deals for the purchasers of retirement homes. We value our independence and can state categorically that we have no affiliation with the vendors of any retirement homes. We do not recommend any specific villages, operators or owners, take no referral fees from retirement home vendors and will not even advertise villages on our website (even though we get numerous requests to do so). For these reasons you can rely on our advice being completely independent and unbiased.

## How to use this book

I assume you are reading this book because either you or a friend or relative are thinking about buying a retirement home. You may even have started your research. I recommend you use this book as a roadmap to show you where to go, what to look for and what questions to ask.

Once you find a retirement community you like, the book will provide a methodology and framework for your research and analysis of how the purchase contract and the different fees and charges work, and what impact they will have on your finances. As you get closer to choosing your retirement home, use the negotiating tips to drive the best deal you can for your purchase. Using the information contained in this book will likely save you thousands of dollars on your retirement home purchase.

First, however, it is important that you identify why you are thinking about buying into a retirement village. Chapter 3 contains information and questions you should consider to help you work out if a retirement village is actually the right move for you. Some people may be better off staying where they are or simply downsizing to a smaller residential property. Chapter 3 will help you make this decision in an objective way.

## How this book is organised

*Don't Buy Your Retirement Home Without Me!* is divided into five parts to make it easier for you to navigate directly to the area where you need assistance.

## Part I: The retirement living industry

In part I, I give you the background and context of the retirement living industry so you can understand why it has grown into such a popular yet confusing sector. I clear up any confusion around what a retirement village actually is and identify the difference between retirement living and aged care. Finally I examine the legal framework that is in place to protect retirement village residents.

## Part II: Assessing your options

In part II, I go through the process of planning your retirement lifestyle and work out if a retirement home is actually the right move for you. Integral to your decision making is deciding *where* to retire, and I discuss some of the issues you need to consider when choosing a location. Finally, I discuss how to assess your capacity to purchase and live in a retirement community.

## Part III: Doing your research

In part III, I get into the nuts and bolts of researching retirement villages and explain how you perform due diligence to work out your best option. I peel back the layers on the types of retirement community homes and how you actually purchase or occupy one. I also provide an overview of retirement village operators—the good, the bad and the ugly.

## Part IV: Analysing your research

I start part IV with an overview of the fees and charges you will encounter and how they actually work. I take you through how to work out if the purchase price of a retirement village unit is reasonable or not, and how to compare different contract structures. I also discuss the impact of capital growth on your purchase and finish by teaching you how to buy a retirement home off the plan in chapter 14.

## Part V: The purchase

I start part V by looking at the decision to sell your existing home. Further material on this subject is available on our website, which I will tell you more about shortly. Next I cover the contract process and explain some of the peculiarities around retirement home purchase contracts. Finally, I teach you how to negotiate your purchase arrangements, and tell you what key terms you should look out for in your contract and how to change these if they are not acceptable to you.

## Part VI: Living and leaving

In part VI, I pass on some practical tips on selecting a removal company and moving house to ensure the least stressful experience for everyone involved. I also look at the best ways to assimilate into your new retirement community and how to keep active and engaged once you are there. Chapter 20 focuses on tools and resources you can access to assist with the whole process.

## Other tools and resources

To provide you with even more assistance, we have set up a members' section on our website, where you can access a range of tools and resources to assist further with your retirement home purchase. On the website you will find the following:

- bonus chapter called 'Selling your home' that provides you with information to help you with:
  - selecting and appointing a real estate agent
  - types of agent appointment
  - driving your real estate agent
  - commissions and fees
  - methods of sale—which one is best and which is appropriate for your home
  - presenting your home for buyer inspections
  - funding presentation work to bring your home up to a saleable condition.
- members' forum where you can ask questions, compare notes and share experiences with other retirees going through the same process
- the Contract Comparison Calculator—an online tool you can use to compare retirement village purchase arrangements
- downloadable copies of the worksheets included in the back of the book, which you can print out in larger format
- free webinars where you can speak directly with the experts at Find My Retirement Home, and find dates and times for the various seminars I present around the country
- video and audio recordings about buying and living in retirement homes
- a question-and-answer forum where your questions can be put to retirement home experts
- a list of accountants, solicitors and financial planners I have trained to assist you with your retirement home purchase
- special discounts and deals.

The Find My Retirement Home members' website is completely free and is an essential tool for your retirement home research. To log on, simply go to the website at <www.findmyretirementhome. com.au> and click on the 'Members' link. This will direct you to log in using your existing username and password or to set up as a new user. Simply follow the prompts to choose a username and use the password 'retire'.

I wish you every success in finding your retirement home and enjoying a healthy, happy and active retirement. Thank you for allowing me to be a part of your journey!

**Richard Andrews**
**Founder and CEO, Find My Retirement Home**

# The retirement living industry

In this part of the book I will look at the evolution of the retirement living industry and how it came to be so confusing. Integral to this is an understanding of the dynamics of our ageing population, which is driving the explosive growth of the retirement living sector. I will wrap up this part by examining exactly what a retirement village is and the legal framework that exists around the country to protect retirement village residents.

# Chapter 1

## The evolution of retirement living in Australia

Up until the 1950s, retirees typically remained in their suburban family home. The house had long been paid off; the kids had left home, married and set up their own families; and Mum and Dad subsisted on their pensions. Wives generally outlived their husbands, who may have been living with physical or mental injuries inflicted by war.

Even today women on average outlive men by several years. When Dad died, Mum would move in with one of the kids, occupying either the spare bedroom or, given the generally smaller house sizes of the time, a traditional Aussie granny flat in the backyard. The granny flat may have been custom-built but was more likely to be a converted garage or garden shed. Outside of the family unit, there were few aged care options; these were mainly hostel- or hospital-style facilities operated by churches or benevolent groups such as the Masons or Returned Services League.

The period leading up to the 1970s saw seniors living longer as a result of medical advances, better quality food and more of it, and a shift in the economy from manufacturing jobs that wore out bodies and minds, to more sedentary, service-based roles.

With a longer period of time now spent in retirement, families were understandably increasingly reluctant to have Nanna living with them at the bottom of the garden for an extended period, and the elderly themselves wanted to live independently for as long as possible. Rising property values also allowed retirees to downsize out of the family home and live comfortably on the proceeds.

Growing demand for retirement communities resulted in many church groups moving into the sector in a big way.

Towards the end of the 1990s, property developers realised there was a fortune to be made from the ageing population and they wanted a piece of the action too. Around this time, state governments began waking up to the impacts of the demographic shift and moved to control the sector through retirement villages legislation.

Since the 1990s the retirement living and aged care industries in Australia have undergone significant changes. Previously the major operators of retirement and aged care facilities had been church groups, charitable organisations, individuals and local authorities. The sector was characterised by rest homes and geriatric hospitals, mostly of fewer than 50 beds.

The retirement living and aged care sectors have experienced increasing demand for quality developments and as a result have undergone significant changes in terms of facility type, ownership and operational structure.

### Key drivers of retirement living sector growth

Key drivers to growth in the sector include:

- an increase in the number of people aged over 60 years
- increased life expectancy
- changes in the lifestyle demands of both the over-65s and their children
- a growing desire for community and socialisation among retirees
- increases in the value of the family home, broadening retirement living options
- growing concerns around security, both personal and property
- changes in the types of facilities available.

The industry of today is very different from that of 20 years ago, with only around half of all complexes owned by the not-for-profits or benevolent institutions. The for-profit operators entered the market in the mid 1980s, but withdrew following the property crash of the late 1980s and early 1990s.

The late 1990s and early 2000s saw the re-entry of corporations, to the extent that between 2000 and 2008 most of the acquisitions of retirement communities or retirement village portfolios were made by listed property trusts and institutional investment vehicles, most of which had not previously been active participants in the sector. This included listed property companies such as Aevum, Lend Lease Prime Life, Becton, FKP, ING and Stockland; and institutional investment vehicles such as the Retirement Villages Group (the largest owner of retirement communities in Australia) and the JP Morgan/Meridien joint venture. As a result of the global financial crisis, these organisations have largely ceased buying and are now focusing on managing their villages and new development pipelines. I talk more about retirement village owners and operators in chapter 8.

The not-for-profit (NFP) sector was largely left behind during the orgiastic feast of consolidation in the latter part of the last decade. However, the planets have now aligned for this group, with market conditions favouring those who had previously missed acquisition opportunities, and the NFPs are now actively expanding their portfolios. Private developers and owners who sold out to institutional buyers in the previous cycle are re-entering the market and are expected to again amalgamate large portfolios.

The entry of profit-focused companies into the retirement living sector has, in my opinion, been good for the industry as a whole. For-profits have brought a level of professionalism, sophistication and market responsiveness that had been lacking with the domination of church and other not-for-profit groups in the sector.

## The ageing population

In this section I look at the population dynamics behind the growth of the retirement living sector. This will provide you with an insight into the impact of the ageing population on domestic housing.

At the time of the nationwide census of 2006 Australians aged over 65 numbered more than 2.7 million and made up around 13 per cent of the population. The retirement industry adopts the age of 65 as the notional point at which a person would normally be eligible to move into a retirement village. In practice, however, the average age at which this move is made is around 70.

As figure 1.1 shows, Australia's aged population is concentrated in the eastern seaboard states, with South Australia and Western Australia also holding reasonable-sized aged populations. Tasmania and the territories have much smaller aged populations.

Figure 1.1: growth in population aged 65+

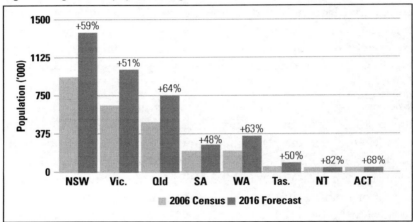

Source: ABS.

Looking forward to 2016, the Australian Bureau of Statistics estimates that this age demographic will grow dramatically in every state, with a nationwide average increase of 54 per cent.

Domestically, as shown in figure 1.2, the 65+ age group will be the fastest growing demographic segment of the population, rising from 13 per cent of the total population in 2006 to 19 per cent in 2026. This represents an increase of 89 per cent over the period, almost four times more than other age groups.

Figure 1.2: 65+ age group as a percentage of the total population

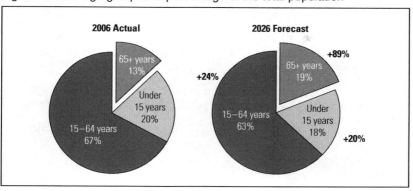

Source: ABS.

The ageing population will present many challenges for governing authorities, but also opportunities for savvy entrepreneurs around the health, aged care, housing and economic impacts of a smaller national workforce.

# Penetration

Now clearly not everyone aged 65+ lives in a retirement village, so in the retirement industry the term penetration is used to measure this. Penetration is the percentage of the population aged over 65 years that actually live in a retirement village. It is estimated that around 5 per cent of Australia's over-65s live in a retirement village, compared with 7 per cent in New Zealand and 13 per cent in the United States. The retirement industry in the US is predominantly a rental model, which is significantly different from our domestic retirement sector. New Zealand, however, has a very similar retirement living model to that found in Australia. The low penetration rate in Australia indicates a future of continuing strong demand for retirement communities.

Colliers International, a respected researcher in the retirement sector, has compiled two penetration forecasts for the Australian market—a Medium Case scenario, in which the rate of penetration growth matches that achieved by the market between 2001 and 2006; and a High Case scenario, in which the penetration increase doubles (see figure 1.3, overleaf).

For the Medium Case, research has shown that the period between 1979 and 2004 saw an annual increase in retirement dwellings of around 5 per cent. If this same rate of increase is maintained, it will result in a penetration rate of 6 per cent of the population aged over 65 years in 2016, and 7.2 per cent in 2026.

Figure 1.3: penetration—percentage of population aged 65+ living in a retirement village

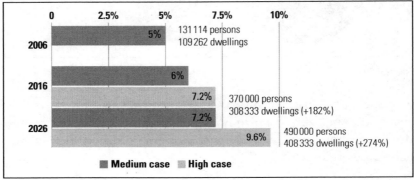

Source: ABS, Colliers.

Although this sounds modest, it results in an increase in actual retirement dwellings of 182 per cent. It is worth noting here that around half the population aged over 65 years is married, therefore a discount of around 20 to 25 per cent is applied to the number of individuals to determine the actual number of dwellings.

For the High Case, the forecast assumes a doubling of the penetration rate between 2016 and 2026. This results in an increase in dwellings of around 270 per cent.

The Medium Case sees Australia equalling New Zealand's penetration rate of 7 per cent by 2026, although still well short of the US precedent of 13 per cent.

The implication of these forecasts is that demand far exceeds the rate of supply, which in basic economic terms means that the pricing initiative is definitely on the side of the seller rather than the buyer. This situation allows the retirement village operator to charge premium prices and higher fees than you would find in a buyers' market.

# Turnover

Retirement village residents will generally stay in their home until such time as they either pass away or require a higher level of care and transfer to a nursing home. The event of a resident leaving a retirement home and the resale of the unit to the next occupant is known in the industry as turnover.

The industry assumes an average length of stay in a retirement village of around 10 years, although anecdotal evidence suggests it is more likely to be seven to eight years.

Turnover is critical to the financial success of most retirement communities, as the operator doesn't actually make any money until a resident leaves the village. The resale of a unit triggers all the fees and charges that have been accruing since the resident moved into the village, as I will explain later.

A retirement village with a high average age across its residents would be expected to have a higher average turnover or, in other words, a shorter average length of stay, than a community with a younger average age. You would therefore be correct in assuming that retirement village operators prefer older occupants, knowing that they are likely to be in residence for a shorter period of time and therefore deliver a faster return.

# Considering average age

It is important that you find a retirement village with an average age of residents that is similar to your own. If you are on the younger side of retirement, you won't want to be stuck in a community full of old people. Similarly, if you are on the higher side of retirement, you won't want to be in a community full of noisy young people! The objective is to find a community of people who want the same things out of life that you do.

Older, or more mature, retirement communities tend to have a higher average age across their residents than newer developments. The ratio of villas and townhouses to apartments also influences the average age, as older residents tend to be attracted to serviced apartments whereas younger, more able-bodied residents prefer houses.

In the next chapter we find out exactly what a retirement village is and the legal framework that exists to protect you as a resident.

## Chapter summary

- The retirement living industry has moved away from being dominated by churches and benevolent groups to becoming a sector that attracts institutional investment from many of the country's largest property groups and investment banks.

- The entry of profit-focused companies into the retirement living sector has been good for the industry as a whole, bringing a level of professionalism, sophistication and market responsiveness that had previously been lacking with the domination of church and other not-for-profit groups.

- Domestically, the 65+ age group is the fastest growing demographic segment of the population, rising from 13 per cent of the total population in 2006 to a predicted 19 per cent in 2026. This represents an increase of 89 per cent over the period, almost four times more than other age groups.

- Penetration refers to the percentage of the population aged over 65 years who actually live in a retirement village (around 5 per cent in Australia).

- The event of a resident leaving a retirement village and the resale of their unit to the next occupant is known in the industry as turnover. The industry assumes an average length of stay in a retirement village of around 10 years.

- Make sure the average age of the residents in your chosen retirement village is close to your own.

# Chapter 2

## What is a retirement village — in legislation and practice?

You will probably have heard a retirement village referred to by many different names, such as over-50s village, independent living resort, retirement community or even lifestyle community. These terms have been introduced by marketers trying to escape the traditional image or stigma of a retirement village — that of an old, depressing suburban complex of boring yellow-brick and chocolate-tile buildings inhabited by the grey cardigan and cup-of-tea brigade. I'll return to that image later. For me the term lifestyle community always conjures up images of nudist colonies! I have actually heard of a proposed nudists' retirement community in the United States, so if that's your thing you may have to move overseas!

In this chapter I will explain what a classic retirement village actually is and how it differs from an aged care facility.

Retirement villages provide accommodation for older, retired people who are largely still able to live independently. Most accommodation options in Australia target the low and middle socioeconomic demographic, with community-style accommodation and additional services such as meals, cleaning or nursing. Further subsectors within the retirement living industry include assisted living units, independent living units and resident-funded villages.

Assisted living units are traditionally small villa- or apartment-style complexes that provide residents with a higher level of on-site care and services and assistance with day-to-day living tasks.

Independent living units (ILUs) are found in age-restricted communities and generally consist of standalone dwellings or apartments that provide accommodation to residents who are independent and require little, if any, assistance with daily living activities. ILUs may also provide an additional range of services on demand such as cleaning, laundry and catering, as well as aged care support services.

In resident-funded villages, residents own a freehold strata-titled property within a complex and pay the full cost of maintenance, management and day-to-day running through ongoing service fees. Any additional services required, such as catering or nursing, must be brought in from external providers such as Meals-on-Wheels or Blue Care.

## The difference between aged care and retirement villages

The retirement living sector is distinct from the aged care sector, which offers aged care or hostel facilities to individuals who can no longer live independently. Most operators of these facilities are not-for-profit entities such as religious or charitable organisations. This is because the current business model for operating aged care allows little or no margin for profit and is therefore largely ignored by for-profit operators. The aged care sector is governed by a single Commonwealth statute that applies across the country, the *Aged Care Act 1997*, whereas retirement homes are operated under various pieces of state and Commonwealth legislation.

To access government-subsidised aged care, an individual must be assessed thoroughly by a health professional who considers all aspects of the person's needs, including physical, medical, psychological and social needs. An Aged Care Assessment Team (ACAT) carries out this assessment, and an aged care facility is unlikely to offer a place to an individual until this assessment has taken place.

If the person has been assessed as requiring aged care and has been offered a place in an aged care facility, a further assessment is made of that person's assets to determine the level of bond or entry fee that is required.

No such assessments are required for residents to access a retirement village. Providing potential retirement village residents are of the required age and can afford the purchase price and on-going fees, there is no reason why they should not be able to buy a residence.

One recent change to the retirement home industry has been the growth of integrated care facilities that offer a range of different care levels in the same location. Such complexes can offer their residents independent living in units, villas or apartments, assisted living in serviced apartments and higher care hospital accommodation. Some retirement village operators have chosen to specialise in one or more of these segments.

## Supported living

Supported living, a blended aged care and retirement village facility, is an increasingly popular model. Supported living is a relatively new concept to Australia that has come out of the United States and is now making significant inroads into the domestic retirement home market.

In supported living facilities, residents live in their own studio, one- or two-bedroom apartments and any care services that are required—from simple cleaning and laundry through to palliative care—are brought to the resident in the home. This differs from most retirement villages that offer aged care in that residents do not have to move out of their independent living unit into an aged care hostel or hospital facility, which under some occupancy contracts can be forced on the resident at the discretion of the village operator. Residents can stay in the comfort of their own home, and couples do not have to separate in the event that one spouse needs a higher level of care than the other.

The supported living concept is becoming the preferred option for people who want to avoid the horrors of Australia's aged care system. Ironically, one of the main reasons why supported living is so successful (for both operators and residents) is that it operates under state retirement villages legislation and not the *Aged Care Act 1997*.

This means that retirees should be able to access the facility without a formal ACAT assessment. However, the facility will usually require a medical assessment so that a care plan can be designed for the resident. Furthermore, no bond payment is required and potential residents do not have to disclose their financial position. Providing they can afford the purchase price (or ingoing contribution) and the ongoing fees, a supported living facility will generally accept them as residents.

---

### Characteristics of supported living

Supported living residences in Australia are a viable alternative to the traditional aged care facility for the following reasons:

- The physical product is significantly better than most aged care hospitals (I would put my mum into a supported living complex, whereas I probably wouldn't be comfortable with her living in a typical nursing home).
- The business model is sustainable for the village operator.
- Couples are not separated if one spouse requires a higher level of care.
- Retirees who lack mobility will experience better social exposure.
- The village operator provides most, if not all, care services on site.
- Care can be delivered to the resident faster and for shorter periods of time than when relying on an external provider.
- Unlike the aged care bond system, the purchase arrangements are market-driven and transparent.

---

## So what is a retirement village?

Legally, a retirement village is defined under the retirement villages legislation in each state and territory. That's right! In another clear demonstration of our inefficient constitutional system, every state and territory has passed its own retirement villages legislation.

Unsurprisingly, though, the legislation across the nation is pretty much the same, with minor differences.

---

Typically, a retirement village is described under the legislation as:

Premises where older members of the community or retired persons reside, or are to reside, in independent living units or serviced units, under a retirement village scheme (*Qld Retirement Villages Act 1999*, Part 1, Div. 3, clause 5.1)

A complex containing residential premises that are predominantly or exclusively occupied, or intended to be predominantly or exclusively occupied, by retired persons who have entered into village contracts with an operator of the complex (*NSW Retirement Villages Act 1999*, Part 1, clause 5 (1) (a))

A community the majority of which is retired persons who are provided with accommodation and services other than services that are provided in a residential care facility; and at least one of whom, before or upon becoming a member of the community, pays or is required to pay an in-going contribution (*Vic. Retirement Villages Act 1986*, Part 1, Sect. 3 Definitions).

---

As you can see, the general thrust of the definitions is that a retirement village provides accommodation for older people under a particular form of scheme or contract.

These schemes or contracts describe an occupancy arrangement that is established predominantly for retirement villages, under which:

- residential units are occupied under a lease or licence
- the right to occupation is conferred by ownership of shares
- residential units are purchased from the administering authority, subject to a right or option of repurchase
- residential units are purchased on conditions restricting their subsequent disposal.

Furthermore, they allow a village owner to structure residents' occupation so that they:

- enter into a residence contract of some sort
- pay a fee to acquire the residence contract
- pay for additional services if required.

In some cases, other legislation applies to the different retirement village legal structures and contractual arrangements, such as state or territory property legislation, strata or community titles legislation, manufactured homes or residential tenancies legislation, or the *Corporations Act* (Commonwealth).

This probably sounds a bit confusing and legalistic at the moment, but stay with me. Later in the book it will become clear which legislation applies to each of the retirement village purchase and occupancy arrangements.

## Retirement village legal framework

Accompanying the rapid growth in the retirement village industry over recent years has been a range of concerns about the way the sector operates and, in particular, how the interests and vulnerabilities of residents are best protected. In response to these concerns the state and territory governments of Australia have passed various pieces of legislation to administer the sector. Because the general intention of the legislation is to provide consumer protection, it is administered by the departments of Fair Trading or Consumer Affairs offices in each state or territory (in South Australia it is administered by the Office for the Ageing).

The consumer protection focus of the legislation means that the power of a village manager to control its relationship with residents is greatest at the time of drafting the underlying contracts, so this is the best time for the purchaser to get it right. To put it another way, once you move into a village, you are stuck with the terms of the purchase contract you signed upon entry. The nature of retirement village contracts means that many of the hidden fees and charges won't bite you on the bum until you exit the village. Unfortunately, retirement village operators do not entertain the defence plea of ignorance at the time of signing!

The retirement villages legislation across all jurisdictions seeks to achieve the following broad principles:

- clarify the rights and obligations of residents and operators of retirement villages

- facilitate the disclosure of all information relevant to a person who is considering entering into a particular retirement village
- require that purchase contracts contain full details of the rights and obligations of the parties
- facilitate resident input into the management of retirement villages, where desired by residents
- establish appropriate mechanisms for the resolution of any disputes between residents and operators.

If you want to find out more about the retirement villages legislation in your state, most administering offices, such as the Department of Fair Trading or Office of Consumer Affairs, publish easy-to-read fact sheets that outline the key points of the legislation. You can download these from their websites or write to them for printed copies.

# Registered and accredited retirement villages

A complex that meets the definition of a retirement village under the state's retirement villages legislation must seek registration by the administering office to ensure formal recognition of its status. Formal government recognition makes a village a registered retirement village.

The owner of a registered retirement village can structure and implement provisions such as granting a lease or licence to occupy the premises, charging ingoing or deferred management fees, applying a no-pets policy and restricting the age of potential residents.

A registered retirement village should not be confused with an accredited retirement village. The Australian Retirement Village Accreditation Scheme is a national accreditation system that seeks to set the minimum benchmark standards for all retirement villages. The Retirement Village Association (RVA), a non-government entity, administers the scheme.

The accreditation scheme sets out a national standards framework and assesses whether villages meet the requirements set. The aim of the scheme is to provide existing and prospective residents, and the wider community as a whole, with confidence that an accredited village is well managed, promotes resident involvement and provides quality services and a safe environment. It provides all stakeholders with a set of best practice standards. Assessments are conducted independently of the village.

The RVA, Australia's peak body for the retirement village industry, has a membership base of more than 600 village and associate members nationally. Membership consists of retirement village operators, managers, owners, developers, investors and industry specialists across Australia. The RVA seeks to enhance the ongoing growth and sustainability of the retirement village industry.

Just to be clear, the RVA is not a government body and it does not represent the interests of village residents. Be careful of using any information provided by the RVA, as their interests are aligned with their members—village owners and operators—rather than with you as a potential retirement village resident.

RVA accreditation can provide a prospective resident with a level of confidence that an accredited village is well managed. As a general rule, however, an ASX-listed retirement village operator with many village sites is a fairly safe bet whether they are accredited or not. If you are considering a retirement community operated by a smaller, unlisted owner-operator with only a few villages, then make sure they have RVA accreditation.

A retirement village can be registered or accredited, or both registered and accredited. The two qualifications represent different criteria, so one is not better than the other.

By now you should have a better idea of what a retirement village actually is, as well as the difference between retirement villages and aged care facilities. In the next part of the book I will investigate the very important question of whether a retirement village is actually the right move for you.

## Chapter summary

- A retirement village is legally defined by the retirement villages legislation in each state and territory.

- The retirement living sector is distinct from the aged care sector, which offers aged care or hostel facilities to individuals who can no longer live independently.

- Integrated retirement facilities offer a range of different care levels within the same location, including independent living in units, villas or apartments, assisted living in serviced apartments and higher care hospital accommodation.

- Under the new supported living model residents live in their own studio, one- or two-bedroom apartments and any care services that are required—from simple cleaning and laundry through to palliative care—are brought to the resident in the home.

- The focus of retirement villages legislation is consumer protection.

- A retirement village provides accommodation for older people under a particular scheme or contract.

- A registered retirement village has been registered under the state's retirement villages legislation and must comply with the legislation.

- An accredited retirement village is one that has been accredited through independent assessment by the Retirement Villages Association, a non-government industry membership group made up of retirement village owners, operators and developers.

# Assessing your options

One of the key decisions for many retired people is whether to stay in their existing home or to downsize to a retirement village or smaller residential property. This decision is often closely related to the financial decisions made around funding your retirement, although many other considerations need to be taken into account as well.

In this part of the book I will discuss in detail the circumstances that make it appropriate for retirees to consider moving out of their existing home. I will then help you assess whether a retirement community would be the right move for you, or whether you would be better off moving to another residential property.

Although these decisions are a source of emotional stress and anxiety for many retirees, answering objective and fact-based questions can help you arrive at the right decision for your particular circumstances.

# Chapter 3

## Working out what you want

Very few people take the time to sit down and plan what kind of lifestyle they want in their retirement. Consequently they find their retirement years lonely, boring and unfulfilling, certainly not what they had dreamt of while slaving away at their jobs over the previous 50 years! Planning your retirement lifestyle not only helps you to maintain an active and engaged routine, it also helps you resolve your accommodation needs.

It is important to plan this decision early in your retirement. You don't want to find yourself forced into a move by circumstances or family members; nor do you want to be under any time pressure to move. You will always achieve a better solution if you have the opportunity to consider carefully all the options available to you.

When I raise this topic with retirees I often find two very different poles of opinion represented: one group assumes that when they retire they are virtually obliged to move into a retirement community, while the other group believes that moving into a retirement community means admitting they are old, and under no circumstances are they going to do that! I find this attitude in particular very frustrating, as it usually means the retiree is going to miss out on the great benefits of retirement community living.

## What does your retirement lifestyle look like?

Planning your retirement lifestyle is essentially planning what you want to do all day during your retirement:

- What activities—hobbies, sports or community involvement— will you pursue?
- How much travel are you planning to undertake? Will it be by rail, road or air?
- How close do you want to be to family and friends?
- How good is your health? Do you need to be close to a particular type of specialist or medical facility?

I encourage you to consider these questions, because once you have mapped out a preferred lifestyle, the subsequent accommodation questions (on location, type of residence, facilities) are logically answered.

In appendix A (see p. 211) you will find a preference questionnaire. This questionnaire has been designed to help you think through the various aspects of location, village and particular residence that are important to you. It is a good tool to use if you are making this very important decision with your spouse or partner, as it helps both of you to articulate exactly what you are looking for in your new retirement home.

The planning process should also provide some answers to the other key questions outlined below. You may have already made some of these decisions, but it is worth going through them in a logical way so you can understand the reasoning behind them.

## Should I stay or should I go?

In other words, should you remain in your existing residence, downsize to a smaller residential property or move into a retirement community?

> ### Moving house — the financial facts
> Financially, you will almost always be better off staying in your existing home, because buying and selling a property incurs fees and charges that can take years of capital growth to offset. Even if your yard is too large and you need to get a mowing service in to do the gardens once a month, or a cleaner to help with the vacuuming, it can still be worth it.

My advice is that you should consider moving only if you:

- are alone or lonely
- fear for your safety or have security concerns about your house or neighbourhood
- don't drive or have access to a car, and public transport is not available nearby
- are bored
- have an older property that is likely to require considerable investment in the future on major items such as roofing, flooring, plumbing or wiring
- are experiencing access issues in your current home, such as a steeply sloping block, steps or multiple levels.

If any of these apply to you, move on to the next question.

You may be wondering why I have not included accessing the equity in your home as a reason for downsizing. For many Australians, most of their wealth is tied up in their home and it is considered logical to access this money by selling the property. But here is the rub — selling your home and moving is stressful and incurs fees such as an agent's selling commission. Buying another home also incurs charges such as stamp duty, which can run into tens of thousands of dollars.

Banks understand this dilemma and many of our financial institutions now offer products such as reverse mortgages by which you can access the equity in your home to fund living or lifestyle costs. One bank actually offers to buy a portion of your home on terms of no interest or repayments until the home is sold. With all of these products, however, you need to consider the costs against the likely capital growth in your home, so you don't go backwards financially. It is best to seek advice from your financial adviser or accountant, who will help you analyse your options.

If you are still paying down the mortgage on your home and are struggling to make the repayments, consider converting the loan to interest only, as this will reduce the payments. Another strategy is to sell or gift a portion of the house equal to the outstanding mortgage amount to a son or daughter and have them assume responsibility for the remaining part of the mortgage. They would assume ownership of the agreed portion of the house and be shown on the title as tenants in common. Again, speak with your accountant or financial planner about these options.

## Should I move into a retirement community or just a smaller house?

The decision whether to move into a retirement community or just into a smaller house is also a complex one. You must understand one very important point, however—a retirement community is about lifestyle. If you are bored, lonely or alone, or fear for your safety, then you should definitely consider a retirement community because it will enrich your life from just about every perspective.

If you already enjoy a busy retirement with a big social network and lots of activities, then you could probably address all your needs simply by moving to a newer, smaller, more secure and better located home. In this case you would also need to be in good health, or have access to an emergency alarm pendant if you are aged in your late seventies or above, so if you have a fall you won't lie injured on your floor for three days until someone finds you.

Try to avoid making this decision based purely on financial considerations because a retirement village will never stack up against a normal, freehold residential property.

The advantages and disadvantages of staying in your existing home are shown in table 3.1.

## Why move into a retirement home?

There is no doubt that most people aged over 65 years prefer to live in their own home as opposed to moving into a retirement village. As outlined in chapter 1, only about 5 per cent of Australia's seniors currently live in a retirement village. It is not known why this figure is so low in comparison with the United States, for example, where about 13 per cent of over-65s live in retirement complexes. Perhaps the difference is cultural—Aussies love home ownership and most retirement complexes in the US are rental accommodation. It is also thought that the standard of retirement living offerings in Australia is not high, and this conclusion has merit when you consider the bland, homogeneous buildings that make up the majority of retirement living villages in this country. The federal government also has a strategy of keeping people in their own homes as long as possible—hence the generous funding for in-home care.

Why, then, do so many retirement communities around the nation have waiting lists of people ready to move in?

Table 3.1: advantages and disadvantages of staying in your existing home

| Advantages | Disadvantages |
| --- | --- |
| Moving incurs transaction fees (stamp duty, sales commissions). | Home too large for current needs. |
| Moving is stressful. | Limited ability to access capital tied up in property. |
| Avoid leaving familiar family home with all its memories. | Less maintenance would be needed in a retirement home. |
| Avoid leaving established community and support networks. | Missed opportunity for a fresh start in a better location. |

People make the decision to move into a retirement village for a number of reasons. Listed here are some of the more common explanations that you may be able to identify with:

* *Neighbourhood.* One of the main reasons people want to move out of their home is because of neighbourhood problems: barking dogs, loud music, hotted-up cars, general noise or changing suburban demographics, such as an influx of immigrants from a particular ethnic group. Retirement communities have rules and restrictions that protect residents from stressful situations, and this is very attractive to seniors. It is not unreasonable to want to live somewhere designed to protect your peace of mind, wellbeing and happiness. It could

also be argued that seniors need more quiet and relief from everyday stress, and this is especially true for those with health problems.

- *Home maintenance.* Maintaining a large family home can be hard work, particularly for older homes. Mowing big yards, especially in the summer, weeding, pruning, watering and painting can take up most of your spare time and prevent you from enjoying those things you had planned to do in retirement. You may also want to travel, and you should be able to do this without worrying about your home — is it secure, who is clearing the mailbox or mowing the lawn while you are away?

- *Downsizing.* People often find that their existing home is too large for them or presents access problems with stairs, narrow access ways or multiple levels, whereas retirement homes are specifically built for easy access and maintenance.

- *Security.* Elderly people are particularly vulnerable to home invasion and if they do not feel safe in their home or neighbourhood, it can cause a great deal of stress.

- *Social life.* Retirement communities are full of like-minded people who generally want the same things out of life that you do. This can make for a busy social life, if that's what you want!

All of these reasons are compelling arguments for you to move into a retirement community.

Table 3.2 shows the advantages and disadvantages of moving into a retirement community instead of a normal residential property.

Table 3.2: advantages and disadvantages of moving into a retirement community

| Advantages | Disadvantages |
|---|---|
| A community of similarly aged and like-minded residents. | Typically a more expensive living option — higher transaction costs. |
| Homes specifically built for low maintenance. | Smaller properties, with little or no backyard. |
| On-site management and, in some cases, meals and medical care. | Limited choice of locations as well as accommodation products. |

| Advantages | Disadvantages |
|---|---|
| Facilities such as gym, pool, clubhouse, village bus. | Generally a poor financial outcome for residents upon exit. |
| Resident restrictions such as minimum age, no pets. | Limited cultural and age variation. |
| Instant social life, friends and activity programs. | Typically no-pets policy. |
| Security and support. | Higher density living—cramped. |

If you don't really have much idea what you want, or if you are basically bored (and this is not unusual for retirees), then a move to a retirement community will certainly kick-start your life again!

### The facts about on-site aged care

In my experience, many people look for a retirement village that offers higher care, so that if they eventually need assistance with daily living tasks, they can simply move out of their unit into the aged care section of the complex. However, this assumption is flawed for these reasons:

- Most villages will require you to sell your unit to fund the move into the aged care facility. The heavy fee structure of most contracts may not leave you with enough money to fund this move.

- The aged care facility may not have any room, and you as a resident may not actually get any preference over outside applicants.

- The in-home care industry is well established in Australia; it is very easy to get care provided in your own home.

## Preference questionnaire

Knowing exactly what you need or want from a retirement community can also be hard to figure out. It is a case of you don't know what you don't know. For example, do you need a hard-standing area next to your unit to park a caravan or boat?

Appendix A (see p. 211) provides a preference questionnaire template that is designed to help you through the process of working out what facilities and services you should be looking for when you start your retirement home research. Complete this form with your family members or trusted advisers before starting your research.

## Chapter summary

- Planning your retirement lifestyle not only helps you to maintain an active and engaged routine, it also helps you resolve your accommodation needs.

- For retirees, the accommodation choices are typically staying where they are or downsizing into a smaller residential property or a retirement community.

- A retirement community is all about lifestyle.

- Only around 5 per cent of Australians aged over 65 live in retirement communities.

- Financially, you will almost always be better off staying in your existing home, because buying and selling a property incurs fees and charges that can take years of capital growth to offset.

- Reasons why people decide to move into a retirement village include:
  - neighbourhood
  - home maintenance
  - downsizing
  - security
  - social life.

# Chapter 4

## Choosing a location

For most retirees choosing a location is simple: typically they want to continue living in the same general location, usually for reasons of family and community. If they decide to change the type of dwelling in which they live — for example, from a larger to a smaller house — or to move into a retirement community, there is a high probability they will purchase a unit in the same general area in which they currently live. The rule of thumb in our cities and larger towns is that around 70 per cent of a retirement village's residents will have previously lived within 10 to 15 kilometres of the complex.

Relocation to other destinations, such as interstate for instance, is more often the result of a desire to be near children and family who have already moved away, rather than the desire for a sea change or tree change experience.

If you are one of the 30 per cent who are keen to pursue a lifestyle option, you are faced with a sea of possibilities.

As far back as 1994 the Australian Bureau of Statistics noted that the highest concentrations of retired people occur in resort/retirement and rural areas. Major concentration areas include the statistical divisions of Moreton (south-east Queensland) and the Richmond–Tweed area on the coastal New South Wales/Queensland border. And with good reason: these areas feature warm climates and an easygoing, laid-back lifestyle. For the retiree, this means the company of like-minded people, as well as a concentration of services that cater to this population demographic.

Interstate migration contributes in large part to this. Unsurprisingly, Queensland nets most of the interstate migrants, followed by New South Wales and Victoria.

Perhaps as global warming increases we will see this situation reverse, with retirees moving south for a cool change.

## Location considerations

When choosing a location, factors for retirees to consider include the following:

- *Affordability.* For most retirees, the ability to fund the purchase of a retirement home depends largely on the sale price of their existing residence, because this is usually the main source of their wealth. Consequently, it would be hard to move from a regional area, such as Wagga Wagga or Wodonga, to a city location, such as Sydney or Melbourne, without a very significant downsizing of your residence in both size and quality. As a general rule of thumb, you can expect to pay more for a unit in a retirement village that is close to the CBD of a major city or town, or in a popular retirement location such as the Gold Coast in Queensland or the Central Coast in New South Wales. Regional cities and towns offer considerably better value, albeit with fewer big-city services, facilities and convenience.

- *Family.* A key consideration for many retirees when choosing a location is proximity to children and grandchildren. At different stages of their lives, individuals feel the need to spend more time with their families, and many choose to move closer to siblings or children. It is a concern, however, when retirees decide to relocate long distances from established friends and community networks to be closer to family members who may have moved away to pursue career or other opportunities. In some cases people have moved interstate to be closer to family members, only to have them move away again when the next career opportunity presented itself, leaving the retiree stranded in a location with no other family members and a limited network of friends. In these situations it is not always easy or financially viable to move again.

- *Climate.* This is also a major consideration. Many retirees relocate to another state seeking a milder climate. For southerners, this may involve moving up to Queensland, whereas northerners may seek to move south to escape the heat and humidity.

- *Health.* Your health is also worth thinking about. Moving out of the city to a regional area may be good for you, with cleaner air and water, less traffic and more sunshine. For retirees in regional or remote areas a key concern may be to live in a more urbanised location with better access to medical facilities.

- *Lifestyle.* Your preferred retirement lifestyle will have a huge impact on your chosen retirement location. If you like water-based activities, such as boating, fishing or swimming, then you need to find somewhere close to a beach or river. If your dream is to have a hobby farm, you can look pretty much anywhere that will allow you to own a few acres and raise some animals.

- *Employment.* For many people these days a retirement lifestyle includes working on a part-time, casual or consulting basis. Retirees may seek out work opportunities to top up their income, keep active or stay engaged in their chosen profession. Some people simply love what they do but want to semi-retire and reduce their working hours. A key consideration for these retirees will be their ability to find the kind of employment they want in their retirement location.

# Retiring overseas

British citizens and Americans are increasingly retiring to locations overseas for a range of reasons — so why hasn't this concept taken off in Australia?

The UK has one of the world's stronger currencies but one of the worst climates! Retired Brits in ever-increasing numbers are heading to continental Europe, where they immediately boost their savings by converting their nest eggs from pounds to euros. Naturally, they head for areas with warmer climates, typically around the Mediterranean — Italy, France, Spain and Greece, as well as Portugal and Croatia. All of these areas are now home to growing enclaves of English retirees who have traded long, damp, nine-month winters for better food, more sunshine and a much lower cost of living.

North American retirees are also fleeing their homeland for southern destinations such as Panama, Costa Rica and the new retiree hotspot of Mexico. Weather is certainly an attraction, but the main reason appears to be financial—lower taxes, a lower cost of living and of course a great exchange rate on their US dollars.

So why don't we see Hawaiian-shirted conga-lines of Aussie retirees heading overseas to live?

For starters, Australia appears to have everything you could ever want in a retirement destination—a first-world, English-speaking nation with clean air and water, mostly crime-free cities and towns, and of course a great climate. How could you possibly improve on that?

Well, it seems you can...

---

### Living the dream

Rob is a 66-year-old who fled Brisbane two years ago after a messy divorce. He has now settled in Hanoi and loves his new expatriate life. 'The cost of living here is about 60 per cent cheaper than in Australia. The people are friendly and I have made some terrific friends from both the local and expatriate communities,' he says.

Rob travels regularly, taking advantage of the cheap flights on offer from the many discount airlines that service Asia. 'Since I have been living in Vietnam I have visited Korea, Japan, China, Malaysia, Cambodia and Laos. I also go to Thailand with friends at least once a month.'

---

## Why retire overseas?

Aussies retire overseas for a variety of reasons, including:

- *Currency.* The Aussie dollar is strong compared with our local neighbours. This positive exchange rate can instantly double or triple your retirement nest egg when converted to a foreign currency. If you are on a pension, this fact alone could significantly enhance your quality of life.

- *Tax.* Australia is one of the highest taxing nations on Earth. There is nothing worse than seeing your hard-earned retirement nest egg decimated by tax-hungry state and federal governments. In contrast, many of our Asian neighbours enjoy low levels of personal taxation.

- *Lower cost of living.* The cost of living in many of our cities is probably about average in comparison with other developed nations but much higher in relation to our Asian neighbours: the report *Mercer's Cost of Living 2010* listed Sydney at number 24 and Melbourne at 33 (with number one being the most expensive). Although ranking below established Asian cities such as Beijing, Tokyo and Seoul, the cost of living in Sydney and Melbourne is more than twice that in Thailand, Malaysia or Vietnam.

- *Climate.* Many people migrate north from the southern states of Australia to enjoy the warmer climes of Queensland in their retirement. Did you know that climates similar to Queensland's are found throughout South-East Asia?

- *Health care.* There is a popular misconception that we have great health care in Australia when compared with third world Asia. Nothing could be further from the truth! Doctors and hospitals in Asia are now so good, and so cheap, that a completely new industry, called medical tourism, has been spawned. In this tourism sector people from expensive developed countries, including Australia, fly to Asia for medical treatment such as plastic surgery or dental work then spend a couple of weeks recuperating by the pool at their luxury hotel. The treatment and two-week holiday, including flights and accommodation, typically cost much less than the price of getting the same procedures performed in Australia.

- *Cheap travel.* If you ever needed convincing about how our domestic airlines overcharge us for air travel, check out the prices of the budget airlines flying out of the major regional ports of Singapore, Hanoi and Kuala Lumpur!

## Overseas retirement destinations

So where are Aussie retirees going? Mainly Malaysia, Thailand, Bali, Vanuatu and New Zealand.

And how do our neighbours feel about Aussie retirees moving to their country? Great! Malaysia even has a government-sponsored program to encourage foreigners to retire in their country.

Retiring overseas can present some downsides, however. Leaving your family to live overseas can be daunting, and abandoning established networks of friends that have taken you years to build is a huge decision. It takes time to settle in a new place — even longer when the language and culture are different.

Still, if you are thinking about retirement locations and yearn for a lifestyle a world away from Aussie suburbia, then trade your local Westfield shopping mall for a fresh produce village market in Asia!

## Pension impacts

Retirees can generally claim an Age Pension only if they live in and are physically present in Australia or a country with which Australia has a negotiated social security agreement. These agreements help to cover gaps in social security coverage for people who migrate between countries. Responsibility for social security is shared between the countries where a person has lived between certain ages, and they may be able to receive pensions from both countries. Usually each country will pay a part pension.

If you are paid an Age Pension in Australia, whether you can continue to be paid, and for how long, if you leave Australia depends on many different factors. These include the country in which you intend to settle, how long you are going for, whether you have only recently returned to live in Australia, and how long you have lived here during your working life.

Because of all the different rules that may affect the decision, it is best to speak with a Centrelink representative as early as possible before your intended departure.

Unless you have returned to live in Australia in the last two years after living overseas, you can generally get the Age Pension for the total period of absence; however, after 26 weeks the rate may change. If you are still outside Australia after 26 weeks, then your normal rate will generally be calculated proportionally, depending on the amount of time you have spent in Australia between the age of 16 and pension age. Centrelink will tell you what proportion is to be used when you advise them of your departure. You will generally need to have lived in Australia for 25 years between these ages in order to receive the full rate. You cannot, however, receive add-ons, such as the Pharmaceutical Allowance or Rent Assistance, if you are living overseas permanently.

If you are thinking about retiring overseas you should contact Centrelink's International Services on 13 1673 to discuss it further.

## Chapter summary

- Most retirees will want to continue to live in the same general location, mainly for reasons of family and community.

- As a rule of thumb for our cities and larger towns, around 70 per cent of a retirement village's residents will have previously lived within 10 to 15 kilometres of the complex.

- When choosing a retirement location, retirees need to consider such issues as family, health, employment opportunities, climate, lifestyle and affordability.

- Retiring overseas can be a great option for retirees who want to increase their quality of life without increasing their spending.

- Australians are now choosing to retire overseas for reasons such as our relatively strong dollar, lower taxes, lower cost of living, better climate, better and cheaper health care, and cheap travel.

- Choosing to retire overseas may affect your eligibility for the Age Pension. Get advice from Centrelink on this before making any decisions.

# Chapter 5

## Affordability

Critical to any decision about your retirement lifestyle, your preferred location and the type of accommodation you want is to work out what you can actually afford. There are two affordability aspects that you will need to consider:

- how much you can afford to spend on your purchase (that is, your purchase capacity)
- your ability to fund the ongoing costs associated with living in a retirement village from your projected retirement income (that is, your spending capacity).

### Purchase capacity

As mentioned already, your ability to fund the purchase of a retirement home will largely depend on the value of your existing home. If you own your home with little or no residual mortgage, then you should be able to afford to buy a retirement home in the same general location in which you live. This is because the prices of retirement village units will typically mirror those in the surrounding residential area. Therefore a two-bedroom villa in a retirement complex should be similar in price to a two-bedroom residential townhouse of similar age and condition in the same suburb. Occasionally a discount of 10 to 15 per cent will apply to the retirement community, owing to the smaller land component, although this is not always the case.

> ### *Pension pitfalls*
>
> Most retirees will have purchased a family home in the city suburbs several decades earlier for little cost, compared with current values. This home, thanks to strong price growth over the occupancy period, is now the main source of their retirement wealth. It is typical for retirees to want to sell this home and purchase a retirement home worth half to two-thirds of the sale value and pocket the difference of several tens or hundreds of thousands of dollars for retirement income or lifestyle expenses. The treatment of this difference does affect your eligibility for the Age Pension, so you need to make sure that you employ the services of a smart accountant or financial planner before you sell your home.

## Valuing the family home

The sale of the family home is an important first step in buying a retirement home, so you need to make sure you get the best price for your home in the best time possible.

Most people have a fairly good grasp of the value of their home, although many of us are emotionally attached to the property and may think it is worth more than it actually is.

There are two ways that you can get a fair indication of the true value of your home for the purposes of working out what you can afford to spend on your new retirement home:

- purchase a sworn valuation from a registered independent valuer
- obtain a Comparative Market Analysis, otherwise known as an appraisal of value, from a real estate agent.

A sworn valuation is a legal document and probably the most professional indication of value you will receive on your property. There are many companies that offer valuations on residential properties and the charge can be anywhere from several hundred dollars to around $1000.

The Comparative Market Analysis (CMA) is an appraisal of value provided by a real estate agent and not a professional, independent valuation. These appraisals can be notoriously variable in accuracy and quality and depend largely on the skill and honesty of the agent. Unfortunately some real estate agents inflate the estimated sale price of your home in the hope of securing the property as a listing for sale, and then spend the sale period trying to talk you down to the real market price of the property! CMAs are provided at no charge so it is a good idea to approach a few agents, rather than just relying on just one. This can be a good first step to finding out the value of the property.

To value a residential property, both professional valuers and real estate agents use the same technique—comparative analysis. This involves analysing the recent sales of comparable properties in the surrounding area to gauge the going market value. This method is highly effective except where there have been no sales of equivalent properties in the previous six to 12 months or where the property is highly distinctive, with unique features not found in comparable properties, such as views, water rights, rural acreages or heritage listing.

All other things being equal, real estate agents should produce a far more accurate value of a property simply because they are operating in the market every day and can draw on more up-to-date information, although this is not always the case. Valuers typically use official data from government sources that may be six months old. If the market is moving quickly—up or down—a CMA from a real estate agent should (in theory) better reflect current value.

## Spending capacity

The second consideration around affordability is your spending capacity, or your ability to fund the ongoing fees and charges associated with living in a retirement community.

First and foremost of these fees is what is known as the general services fee, weekly fee or village fee, which is charged to the residents of most types of retirement villages. The fee is an ongoing charge to the resident and covers the costs associated with running the village, including security, maintenance, management and landscaping. It is similar to the body corporate or owners corporation fee paid by the residents of strata-titled communities such as apartment buildings and is levied on either a weekly, fortnightly or monthly basis. This fee is covered in more detail in chapter 11.

The benchmark I use for a village fee is $100 per week, although it may be higher if the community has extensive facilities such as bowling greens, pools or a clubhouse. It is also higher in leasehold villages because a component of rent for the plot of land is incorporated into the fee, although the lease amount itself may be offset by a resident's eligibility for the Rent Assistance allowance from Centrelink. Village owners know that their residents are on a pension, so it is unlikely you will find a village with excessive ongoing fees because residents simply cannot afford them.

The ability of retirement village residents to fund ongoing village fees is limited, because many of them rely on a pension for their daily living costs or are perhaps self-funded from investments. Either way there is usually not an excess of cash available to fund the village fee. Consequently some village operators charge a lower village fee and offset high operating costs by applying a higher exit fee (more about this later). For example, a particular village might have a justifiable levy on a unit of $135 per week, but instead charge $90 per week and add 10 per cent to the exit fee calculation to make up the difference over time. This is a perfectly reasonable way of providing access to potential residents who have limited incomes but may be asset-rich from the sale of their home.

To assess your capacity to fund the village fee, you will need to forecast your retirement income from all sources and determine what you can afford to pay on an ongoing basis. It is best to use a smart accountant or financial planner to assist you with this work, as you may also be eligible for the Rent Assistance allowance, which may help offset part of the village fee.

### The living cost comparison

It is worth comparing the ongoing costs associated with living in a retirement village (the living expenses) with the costs you would incur by staying in your own home. A typical family home in the suburbs would attract rates and utilities of around $3000 per year. Add to this your home insurance (not including your contents insurance—you will still need this in a retirement village) of perhaps $500 to $1000, as well as an estimate for annual maintenance (higher for older homes). Compare this with your village fee of $5000 to $6000 per year and you will find that the cost of living in a retirement village is roughly similar, or perhaps only slightly higher, than staying in your own home, but without all of the headaches!

## Chapter summary

- Determining your ability to afford a unit in a retirement community requires an assessment of:
  - how much you can afford to spend on your purchase (your purchase capacity)
  - your ability to fund the ongoing costs associated with living in a retirement village from your projected retirement income (your spending capacity).
- Your purchase capacity is usually related to the value of your home and what you will realise from the sale of this property.

# PART III

# Doing your research

So far in the book I have explained what retirement villages are and the legal framework that is in place to protect you as the resident. We have looked at some of the most popular reasons why people move into retirement villages and also discussed the importance of planning your retirement lifestyle. I introduced the concept of retiring overseas and outlined how you assess your ability to purchase and fund a home in a retirement community.

In part III, I get into the detail of how to research retirement villages. Then, in part IV, I will explain how to analyse your findings.

# Chapter 6
## Retirement home research

When making a purchasing decision that involves a lot of money, such as buying a home, it is important to do thorough research, or what property experts call due diligence. Buying a retirement home is no different. In fact, because of the complexity of the transaction and the variety of fees and charges that apply, due diligence is even more important before reaching a decision on a retirement home.

In this chapter I guide you through a step-by-step process that will help you to find the right retirement home for your situation, as well as negotiate the best deal you can on the purchase contract. The process I will outline is exactly what I use to help my clients at Find My Retirement Home.

Figure 6.1 illustrates the due diligence process for researching your ideal retirement home.

Figure 6.1: retirement home due diligence process

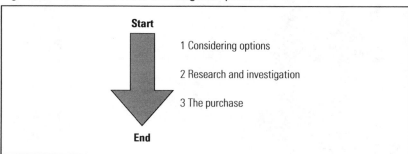

## Considering your options

People will typically first start thinking about purchasing a retirement home in their mid to late sixties while they are still working or once they have retired. I covered the reasons why people move into a retirement home in chapter 3. In the early decision-making stages people are usually beginning to think about the size of their house and the ongoing maintenance required, or wanting to travel without having to worry about the security of their home. Another important consideration is health and perhaps the need for ongoing medical assistance.

It is typical for retirees to delay making this momentous decision, and take time to discuss it with family, friends and trusted advisers such as a financial planner, accountant or solicitor. You may also be under pressure from family members who are concerned for your wellbeing. It is important that you make the move on your terms and in your own time, but before the move is forced on you by circumstances.

Figure 6.2 sets out the key questions to be resolved before starting your research.

Figure 6.2: key questions around your retirement decisions

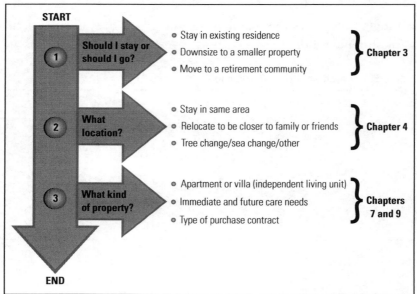

Questions 1 and 2 have been covered in previous chapters. Question 3 will be covered in the next two chapters.

# Research and investigation

Six to twelve months after first thinking about the move, the retiree may actually start looking around for a retirement home. They will typically begin their search in their local area or perhaps where they have enjoyed holidays in the past. They may do a few site inspections and collect a few sales kits. Around this time they start to grasp the complexities of the sector and are introduced to such delights as purchase contracts and exit fees. At this stage, unfortunately, it is not unusual for retirees to put off the decision to move or simply abandon the idea, particularly if they are alone and perhaps do not have people they trust to assist or advise them.

The reality is that many people, daunted by the bewildering process before them, will put off the decision to move into a retirement home until an event, such as a serious fall or the death of a spouse, prompts the change. Such an event creates immediate pressure to move, which forces people to make decisions that may not actually deliver the best outcome for them. As a result, they may sign up to contracts they do not fully understand and will probably pay more than they should.

## Gathering information

The first stage of the research and investigation process is gathering information, in which you assemble information on the retirement village options in your locations of choice. This is not as daunting as it sounds. The individual village questionnaire in appendix B (see p. 217) sets out all the questions you need to ask. Your findings from these sheets can then be summarised in the research comparison worksheet in appendix C (see p. 221).

From your reading in part II, you should now have a good idea of your preferred retirement location. You begin your research by compiling a comprehensive list of every retirement village in your preferred location to compare what is on offer.

## Making your list

If you do not have access to a computer, then your best option is to draw up a list from the local Yellow Pages. Most retirement villages advertise in the Yellow Pages, so this is a good place to start.

If you do have access to the internet, there are lots of online retirement village directories you can use to help with the search. These directories store the details of many retirement villages and act as search engines so you can find the retirement communities in your preferred locations.

> ### Retirement village online search directories
> Good online retirement village directories include:
> - <www.yellowpages.com.au>
> - <www.seniorlivingonline.com.au>
> - <www.seniorshousingonline.com.au>
> - <www.retirementlivingonline.com.au>
> - <www.itsyourlife.com.au>
> - <www.villages.com.au>
> - <www.rva.com.au>.

It is a good idea to use more than one search directory as well as the Yellow Pages, because some villages are only listed on certain websites. All of these directories charge the retirement village a fee to list on their site, so none of the sites offer comprehensive coverage of every option available in a particular area. The larger retirement village owner-operators (see chapter 8 for a review of these organisations) have their own branded websites with search engines for their own portfolio of villages. Independent retirement villages or owner-operators with only one or two villages may not have a website at all, or their site may be limited, lacking good, up-to-date information.

Alternatively you can conduct a search using your favourite general search engine, such as Google, Bing or Yahoo, by entering the keywords 'retirement home' and then your preferred location. For example, 'retirement village central coast nsw'.

From the results of your search, you should now be able to make a list of all the villages in your preferred location. At this early stage, do not exclude any village unless it is very obviously not going to meet the criteria you identified in the preference questionnaire in appendix A on p. 211 (for example, the village is in the CBD and you want something near the beach). As a preliminary step, a simple drive by of each village on the list is a good way to get a feel for the general location and aspect. From this exercise you may start crossing off sites that are clearly not going to meet the criteria you identified in the preference questionnaire.

# Researching your list

You now have a shortlist of villages that warrant further investigation. To research this list you will need to use the individual village questionnaire (see appendix B on p. 217) and the research comparison worksheet (see appendix C on p. 221). If you would prefer a larger version of these worksheets or want more copies, you can download them from the members' section of our website at <www.findmyretirementhome.com.au> using the password noted in the introduction. Here you will also find short videos on how to use these worksheets, if you need more help to fill them out.

## Individual village questionnaire

The individual village questionnaire (an example is shown in figure 6.3, overleaf) is simply a list of the key questions that you need to ask when researching a retirement village, presented in a handy worksheet that you can use to record your answers. Using one worksheet per village, write the village name at the top of the sheet and then begin to fill out the questions along the left-hand side of the page. You should be able to find some of the information simply from your internet searches and online retirement village brochures.

An important part of your research on a retirement village is to review the disclosure statement. In chapter 16 I explain what a disclosure statement is and what information it needs to include. I also outline additional information that I think you should ask for, so make sure you include these questions in your research.

Figure 6.3: example of part of an individual village questionnaire

| INDIVIDUAL VILLAGE QUESTIONNAIRE | | |
|---|---|---|
| **Village:** | | Boronia Garden Village, Boronia Heights |
| **Date Inspected:** | | Jun-12 |
| **COMPLEX SUMMARY:** | | |
| Address | | 30-45 Eastwood Rd, Boronia Heights |
| Postcode | | 2240 |
| Telephone | | 02 9562 1233 |
| Website | | www.boronia-gardens.com.au |
| Operator / Owner | | Private company |
| Registered Retirement Village | Y/N | Y |
| Accredited Retirement Village | Y/N | Y |
| Year Constructed | | 2000 |
| Avg. Age of Residents | | 78 |
| Avg. Time in residence | Years | 4.5 yrs |
| Avg Sale time | Months | 5 months |
| No. Units in Village | | 100 |
| No. of Vacancies | | 25 |
| Pool | Y/N | Y |
| Club house | Y/N | Y |
| Bowling Green | Y/N | N |
| Pets | Y/N | N |

## Research comparison worksheet

The research comparison worksheet (as shown in figure 6.4) is where we log all the information from the individual village questionnaires into a single document so we can compare and contrast the villages. To complete this worksheet, provided in appendix C (see p. 221), you enter the shortlisted villages along the top row and record your research results under each village going down the page using the data you have sourced for your individual village questionnaires. This worksheet is designed to help you easily and quickly compare the various services, facilities, fees and location attributes of your shortlisted communities.

Figure 6.4: example of part of a research comparison worksheet

| RESEARCH COMPARISON WORKSHEET | | | | |
|---|---|---|---|---|
| **Villages:** | | Boronia Village | Eastcliffs | Covent Garden Village |
| **LOCATION SUMMARY:** | | | | |
| Suburb | | Boronia Heights | Eden | Ormeau |
| Postcode | | 4203 | 4275 | 4208 |
| Median Unit Price | $ | n/a | $628,000 | $462,000 |
| Last 12 Months Cap Growth (units) | % | n/a | 14.4% | 8.9% |
| Avg Cap Growth last 10 yrs (units) | % | n/a | 12.2% | 7.7% |
| Median House Price | $ | $525,000 | $700,000 | $603,000 |
| Last 12 Months Cap Growth (houses) | % | 12.3% | 14.4% | 10.0% |
| Avg Cap Growth last 10 yrs (houses) | % | 10.8% | 10.4% | 9.8% |
| Capital Growth Forecast - 10 yrs | % | tba | tba | tba |
| **COMPLEX SUMMARY:** | | | | |
| Address | | 61 Explorer Drive | 19 Banchory Court | 148 Smith St |
| Telephone | | 13 28 36 | 13 28 36 | 13 28 36 |
| Website | | http://www.boroniavillage.com.au | http://www.edenvillage.com.au | http://www.coventgardensvillage.com.au |
| Contact | | Peter | Margaret | Sally |
| Operator / Owner | | Aveo | Primelife | Carlyle |
| Registered Retirement Village | (Y/N) | Yes | Yes | Yes |

To find all the information required for the individual village questionnaires and research comparison worksheet, you will need to start communicating directly with the villages. This can be done in person by visiting the sites or by telephoning them. Telephone calls are probably the best method in the first instance, but you should be careful of villages that try to avoid your questions by offering to send out a brochure pack. There is no harm in receiving brochure packs; however, you will end up swimming in paperwork given the volume of information that some sales agents like to send! Also note that brochure packs rarely answer even half the questions listed on the worksheets.

From the research you have done so far you will be in no doubt that some villages, for whatever reason, are not going to be suitable, and these properties can now be excluded from any further research. For the villages that have made the cut, now is the time to do a personal inspection. The depth and time spent on a personal inspection depends on you—some people will make a fast decision, whereas others may need to visit a community several times before deciding.

---

### *Inspecting a retirement village*

Here are some suggestions for personal inspections:

- Ask to inspect occupied homes as well as vacant ones. This will help you to visualise what a property will look like when it is occupied, as empty residences can appear larger than they actually are.

- Ask to meet some of the residents so you can question them on what they like or don't like about the village.

- Have a meal in the dining room to check out the food (if applicable).

- Ask if you can stay for a night or two at the village. Some complexes are set up for this and are more than happy to accommodate potential residents.

---

So what are you looking for on your personal inspection? Here is a list of my suggestions to get you started:

- Are the common areas clean and well maintained?

- Does it look as though the owner of the village reinvests profits into the facilities?

- Are the facilities in good repair?

- Are the existing residents house proud—do they care for their properties?

- Do things work? For example, are there out-of-order signs on lifts, pools or spas?

- Is there a buzz about the place—do the residents look happy?

- Is there evidence of an active social life in the complex? Ask to see the social calendar.

- Are the gardens and landscaping well maintained or overgrown and unkempt?

- Do the on-site manager and staff appear to like their jobs? Speak to them, if you can. What is staff turnover like?

Make sure you record your impressions by taking detailed notes, as you will no doubt become confused once you have looked at more than one village. It also makes it easier to evaluate your data at a later date.

# The purchase

The uniqueness of retirement home purchase contracts unfortunately means that a purchase is more complex than the standard residential property purchase with which you may be familiar.

The purchasing decision should be made only after evaluating and considering all the information you have gathered from your research. By now either you will have a pretty good idea of which retirement village is your preferred option or you will be more confused than ever!

In part IV, I will show you how to analyse the information you have collated through your research. Then, in part V, I will take you through the components of a retirement home purchase.

# Chapter summary

- When making an important purchasing decision with high cost ramifications, such as buying a home, it is important to do thorough research, or due diligence.
- The due diligence process consists of:
  - considering options
  - research and investigation
  - the purchase.
- The key questions that must be answered at the considering options stage include:
  - Should you stay in your existing residence or downsize to a smaller property or retirement community?
  - Where do you want to live?
  - What type of retirement home is going to be most appropriate to your retirement lifestyle and future needs?
- Retirees will typically put off the decision to move, and it often takes an event such as a serious fall or the death of a spouse to trigger the change. Such an event creates immediate pressure to move, which forces people to make retirement home decisions

that may not actually deliver the best outcome for them, and they will probably to pay more than they have to.

- Gathering information on potential retirement homes is easy if you use the individual village questionnaire and research comparison worksheets in the appendices.
- Retirement village purchase contracts are more complex than standard property purchase contracts.

# Chapter 7
## Types of retirement accommodation

When you start researching retirement villages you may be overwhelmed by the variety of accommodation options available to you—the number of rooms, the size, the style, and so on. New developments are also devising their own names for the different types of residences they are building. For example, a new retirement village development may build a villa-style house they call a Boronia. The Boronia A-type may feature a one-car garage, while the Boronia B-type has a two-car garage.

Put simply, there are basically only two types of retirement housing—an independent living unit, or ILU in industry-speak, and a serviced apartment. An ILU can be a villa, similar to a one-level townhouse, or an apartment. A serviced apartment is simply an apartment!

Figure 7.1 shows the types of retirement accommodation and their relationship to the level of care offered.

Figure 7.1: types of retirement accommodation and levels of care

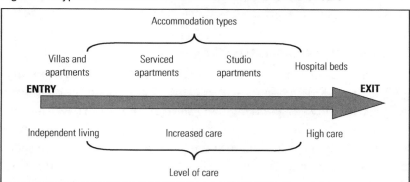

If you are like most retirees, you are probably uncomfortable discussing your health and believe you will live forever! As a rule of thumb, if you are in your mid to late seventies or older, you should consider retirement villages that offer increased care services. If you are between the ages of 55 and 75 and in pretty good health, then it is likely you can afford to be more flexible in your choice of village and select a complex with no internal care provisions.

The best solution is for you to remain in one location for as long as possible. Later in the book I will demonstrate the impact that length of tenure can have on the financial outcome of your retirement home purchase.

Modern retirement living communities offer a mix of accommodation styles and care options. This allows the village owner to manage residents within the complex as their needs increase. For example, a resident may initially move into an independent living villa or townhouse within the community. As their independence and mobility decrease, they have the option to move into a smaller, more easily maintained apartment also within the community. This is a great option for residents as they are able to increase their levels of care without leaving the community and their friends.

There are downsides to this strategy. Many retirement home purchase contracts include clauses that allow the village manager to force the resident to move into the higher care option. In addition, the resident has to execute an exit and resale of their independent living unit and purchase an aged care unit, a process that has considerable financial implications for the resident. Another problem can be the lack of available beds in the aged care facility—you may have to go onto a waiting list.

## Villas and apartments

Villas and the larger, two- and three-bedroom apartments are popular with mobile, independent retirees. This type of accommodation is designed for fully independent living and can range from basic through to luxury living. These purpose-built residences are not dissimilar to standard residential housing, although they feature special retirement living fittings such as enhanced security, emergency call buttons for medical assistance, wider doorways and larger shower cubicles.

Residents of independent living units have access to all the community facilities within the complex. These units are typically unserviced—that is, care and other services are not automatically provided—although residents can purchase services such as cleaning or personal care for an additional fee.

Villas and apartments are most popular with retirees in good health, with most aged between 71 and 85 years when they first buy a retirement residence. These individuals are mobile and don't require assistance with daily living tasks.

Independent living units are typically sold to residents under a freehold, leasehold or deferred management fee purchase structure.

## Serviced apartments

Serviced apartments are smaller than ILUs and offer an enhanced level of care. The resident will pay a higher general services or village fee and receive services such as cleaning, meals and laundry.

Serviced apartments are designed to provide a level of personal care within a residential environment to individuals who can no longer cope with some daily tasks on their own. Typically these residents require assistance in one or more activities of daily living including housework, shopping, meal preparation and, in some cases, personal care. We categorise these residents as being in the middle continuum of care, between independent living and an aged care home. They are typically aged 75 years and over.

As their mobility and independence decrease, residents currently living in independent living units may seek to relocate within the retirement community to a serviced apartment for the increased level of care it offers.

## Studio apartments or hospital rooms (high-care facilities)

The third style of accommodation is the studio apartment, which is similar to a private hospital room. These units, popular with residents requiring close medical supervision, are generally located in a hospital wing within the village and offer 24–hour medical care.

Potential residents of independent living units take comfort from the close proximity of higher care facilities within the complex, reassured that they will not have to relocate to another facility in the future as their mobility and independence decrease. This provides a kind of psychological safety net, similar to having a medical centre next door.

Sometimes one spouse requires a higher level of care than the other. A community that offers a range of living options across the care continuum allows couples to stay together as long as possible.

The higher care facilities are usually designed to be private and discrete from the independent living areas frequented by able-bodied residents.

Villages that offer a higher care arrangement will typically do so only in a limited way, unless they specialise in this service. This is because there is little profit in higher care and the service is included mainly as a selling feature to attract buyers for the independent living units, from which retirement village operators make most of their money.

## Chapter summary

The three styles of accommodation typically available in retirement villages are independent living units, serviced apartments, and studio apartments or hospital rooms:

- Independent living units, or ILUs, are villa-style properties or larger apartments designed for residents who require little if any assistance with daily tasks.
- Serviced apartments are smaller units that offer assistance to residents with some daily tasks such as cleaning or meal preparation.
- Studio apartments or hospital rooms are similar to a private room at a hospital and accommodate residents who require constant medical supervision.

# Chapter 8
## Retirement village operators

The company that operates your village can have a big impact on your overall experience. When you start investigating potential communities you will likely be amazed at the vast range of different retirement village brands, owners and operators.

Basically, however, there are only two types of retirement village operators—not-for-profit organisations, or NFPs, and for-profit companies. For-profit companies can be further divided into private companies and public companies that are listed on the Australian Securities Exchange (ASX).

As I discussed in chapter 1, the retirement village industry was originally started up by NFP organisations, including church groups and benevolent societies, such as the Masons and the Returned Services League. The market is rapidly consolidating, however, with the entry of banks and property companies, and the corporatisation of retirement village management. It is estimated that large for-profit industry operators now account for roughly 50 per cent of the market, with the remaining properties owned by NFPs and smaller, privately owned enterprises.

Benefits brought to the sector by the for-profits include:

- The departure fee model, under which most homes in retirement communities are sold in this country, requires a village owner to have a strong balance sheet owing to the volatile nature of the cash flows from this kind of business. The large for-profit operators are conservatively geared (at least they are now, post-GFC!) and can provide balance sheet stability.

- The larger retirement village owner-operators are listed on the ASX. As a result, retirement village residents and the general public can access detailed financial and operational information about the company, whereas private and not-for-profit operators have no public disclosure obligations and you will never know how strong or precarious their financial situation is until it is too late.

- The large, listed retirement village owner-operators are extremely averse to negative publicity, as this can adversely affect their share price. This makes them a little more motivated to resolve disputes with residents so they don't end up as the headline story on a current affairs show! It is also easy for disgruntled residents to acquire shares and confront the company's directors at general meetings.

- Larger organisations are able to pay their executives more money and—in theory, at least—should therefore attract a better quality executive.

- Larger operators should be able to discount retirement village units in the lean times to make sales, knowing they can claw this money back on the subsequent resale of the unit. Smaller operators are more hesitant or simply unable to do this, as they need the cash.

- Larger operators can provide better systems and training for village sales staff and managers.

- Larger operators have less chance of going broke, reducing those situations where retirement village residents are turfed out of their homes.

## For-profit operators

Table 8.1 lists some of the major for-profit retirement village operators in Australia.

Table 8.1: for-profit retirement village operators

| Company | Details |
|---|---|
| Becton Retirement Living | ASX-listed property developer and owner-operator of retirement villages. |
| FKP | ASX-listed property developer and owner-operator of retirement villages; managed under the Aveo brand. |
| Hindmarsh Living | Property developer now specialising in the development and operation of retirement villages, predominantly in Canberra. |
| ING | Big global bank that operates a portfolio of retirement villages in Australia under the Settlers and Garden Villages brands. |
| Lend Lease | ASX-listed owner-operator of retirement villages; managed under the Primelife and Retirement by Design brands. |
| Living Choice | Private property developer now focused on retirement villages. |
| Meridien | Private property development company that owns and operates retirement villages under the Meridien brand. |
| RVG (FKP/ Macquarie Bank joint venture) | Unlisted retirement trust made up of superannuation funds and other institutional investors; largest owner of villages in the country; managed by FKP under the Aveo brand. |
| Rylands | Private, high-end operator of retirement villages in Victoria. |
| Stockland | ASX-listed trust that owns and operates retirement villages; recently took over the ASX-listed Aevum Group. |
| TriCare | Private company operating aged care and retirement living facilities in Queensland |

## Not-for-profit operators

Table 8.2 lists some of the major not–for–profit retirement village operators in Australia.

Table 8.2: not-for-profit retirement village operators

| Company | Details |
| --- | --- |
| Anglicare | National network of Anglican organisations providing retirement living and aged care, among many other services. |
| Baptist Care | Western Australian-based NFP run by the Baptist Church. |
| Blue Care | Formerly known as the 'Blue Nurses', this group now develops and operates retirement villages around Australia. |
| Churches of Christ Care | Religious group operating retirement communities and aged care facilities within Queensland. |
| Masonic Homes | Large operator of retirement living and aged care residences around the country. |
| RSL Care | Runs 27 retirement communities throughout Queensland and New South Wales. |
| Southern Cross Care | One of the largest aged care providers in the country. |

It is hard to generalise about the best owners–operators of retirement villages, as they are all very different. On one hand, it would seem self-evident that NFPs have your best interests at heart because they are, well, not-for-profit. However, we can assume that NFPs do try to make money from their operations to fund other social ministries supporting the community that don't make money.

It could also be argued that NFPs are not always as efficiently run as for–profit organisations, and they certainly don't attract the same quality of executive as a Lend Lease, FKP or Stockland. The larger, listed companies are also very sensitive to adverse publicity and are likely to be more responsive to resident concerns. One of the other advantages of selecting a large listed company as your village operator is the fact that its financial strength is publicly available for you to review. ASX listing rules require that organisations lodge their financial statements regularly, so you can check issues such as their corporate strategy and levels of debt. Private companies and not-for-profit organisations have no public disclosure requirements, so you will never know if they are about to go broke.

NFP retirement villages associated with a particular religion (such as Churches of Christ Care) or group (such as RSL Care) typically accept residents whether or not they are members of their particular church or organisation. For example, you don't have to be a returned serviceman to buy into an RSL Care village. Some of the church-affiliated villages feature Sunday services on site, but residents are under no obligation to attend. However, to avoid discord you should consider choosing a retirement village operator with a philosophy that is similar to your own. For example, it would be best not to buy into a church-based village if you are an atheist!

As a very general rule, I recommend that you seek answers to the following questions when selecting your village owner-operator:

- Does the retirement village owner-operator have a strong balance sheet (i.e. no more than 30 per cent debt as a proportion of its assets)?
- Is retirement living its core business?
- Is it in the retirement living business for the long term, or is it simply a residential developer having a go at retirement villages?
- Is there a corporate/head office structure dedicated to the retirement living business sitting behind the on-site village management?
- Is it too focused on expanding its portfolio by developing new communities?

It is worth noting that your day-to-day experience in a retirement village is more likely to be influenced by the village manager and residents, regardless of who owns or operates the village.

## Not for profit? Not necessarily!

Many people are attracted to the idea of living in a retirement community operated by a not-for-profit organisation (NFP) because they are confident they will not be ripped off. After all, you can trust a not-for-profit organisation, can't you?

Is this necessarily the case? The retirement home sector was traditionally dominated by NFPs such as church groups and charitable associations. Over the past decade, however, the sector has attracted significant interest from for-profits such as investment banks and property companies, to the extent that more than half of the retirement villages in the country are now owned by the for-profits.

It could be argued that NFPs were originally motivated by a strong sense of 'mission' in building their portfolios of retirement village assets. In fact, the much-maligned deferred management fee scheme was created by the NFP sector, which discounted a property by 20 to 30 per cent of the market value to allow struggling retirees to purchase a unit and then made this discount back via the deferred management fee when the resident departed the complex.

Today, however, there is no difference between the purchase contracts offered by NFPs and for-profits. Both use deferred management fee schemes with great effect to their bottom lines. Some NFPs do allocate a portion of their community to subsidised housing, although this is the exception rather than the rule.

## Chapter summary

- Large corporations own a large percentage of the retirement villages in Australia, with the remainder owned by not-for-profits (NFPs) and private companies.

- Not-for-profit retirement village operators use the same contracts as for-profit operators, so you should not expect to get a better deal from the NFP operators.

- Although it is important who the operator of your retirement village is, in reality the village manager and other residents will have a greater impact on your experience of living in the retirement village.

# Chapter 9

## Retirement home purchase arrangements

Retirement home purchases are arranged in many different ways, and this creates one of the biggest sources of confusion for retirees. In this chapter I will explain all the purchase arrangements that apply to retirement villages in Australia, so you can identify the characteristics of each type when you start your research. Each purchase option has its own benefits and disadvantages, which I will outline in detail.

In an ideal world, you would be able to choose the purchase option that best suits your personal circumstances or intentions; however, this is rarely the case. In practice, the purchase arrangement used by a village will be a secondary consideration—it is more important that you find the right retirement community in the right location.

In Australia there are five ways that a retiree can purchase or occupy a unit in a retirement village. It is not unusual to find variations within each type of arrangement, particularly between different states and territories.

The five different types of arrangements are:

- freehold (typically in a strata-titled community)
- leasehold
- company title
- rental
- the deferred management fee or DMF scheme, also known as loan/licence or loan/lease.

# Freehold

Freehold properties are found within strata-titled communities. The purchase process is similar to any freehold property purchase that uses a community title scheme, such as a block of units or townhouses. From a retirement living perspective, these properties are generally located in a complex that may be registered as a retirement village under state legislation and is exclusive to a particular age group such as over-55s. A regular body corporate or owners corporation fee is charged to residents, typically on a quarterly basis, and covers the expenses associated with the operation of the community including grounds, maintenance, on-site management, security and insurance.

Occasionally the freehold retirement village by-laws will permit unit owners to rent out their property if they choose, provided the tenant complies with the village covenants regarding age. But this arrangement is unusual and most retirement villages, whether freehold or not, have strict owner-occupier provisions.

Within strata-titled freehold retirement villages there is a body corporate or owners corporation that governs the complex within the limits of the body corporate charter and the relevant state or territory community titles legislation. The owners corporation is run by a committee made up of unit owners who hold the various positions of office such as chairperson, treasurer and secretary.

It is not unheard of for banks to provide finance to residents wishing to purchase a unit in a freehold retirement village, because the freehold title can be mortgaged. Typically, if you own your home outright you should not need finance; however, it is a useful piece of knowledge to keep up your sleeve, perhaps if you need bridging finance to settle on a retirement home before the sale of your own home.

As you can see in table 9.1, some of the strengths of the freehold purchase arrangement are also weaknesses, such as the fact that resales and refurbishments are the responsibility of the resident. Some purchasers appreciate having full control these issues, whereas other people prefer to have the village operator look after resales and refurbishments on their behalf.

Table 9.1: freehold strengths and weaknesses

| Strengths | Weaknesses |
|---|---|
| Freehold title owned by the resident. | Usually limited or no facilities (for example, no pool). |
| Security of tenure. | No third party manager—an owners' committee runs the complex. |
| No third party manager—an owners' committee runs the complex. | Typically built by developers who have no interest in the long-term health or viability of the complex. |
| Resale is managed by the resident. | Resales managed by the resident. |
| Superior financial outcome at end of occupation. | Refurbishments (if required) managed by the resident. |
| Exclusivity—strata freehold is rare and popular with retirees. | Rare, hard to find. |
| Resident discretion to refurbish for resale. | Are typically villa-style, not apartments. |
| No exit fees. | More expensive. |

### Freehold falsehoods

Be careful of retirement villages that tout themselves as freehold but still charge the resident fees normally applicable to the deferred management fee scheme, such as exit fees. In promoting the freehold idea the village operator seeks to convince you that you have greater control over your unit (you really don't) or better security of tenure (debatable). In fact, these villages end up costing you more because of the stamp duty you must pay to your state government on purchase.

True freehold villages are free of exit fees and will provide you with the best financial outcome of all retirement village purchase arrangements. Unfortunately very few of them exist.

# Leasehold

Leasehold is another type of purchase arrangement. It should not be confused with the loan/lease arrangements that I refer to in the book under the deferred management fee model. Under a leasehold arrangement the resident owns the house and leases the plot of land from the village operator. The house may be a brick-and-tile on slab building or a movable structure, such as a prefabricated home.

The resident pays an ongoing body corporate or owners corporation fee that covers costs such as the lease payment, rates, and grounds and maintenance. If you are on a pension, you may be able to claim the Rental Assistance allowance against the rental part of the weekly fee, which could be around $40 per week. Check with your financial planner or Centrelink office for information regarding this benefit.

Under variations of this scheme, exit fees may or may not apply, although typically they do not.

Most leasehold villages are pitched at the cheaper end of the market and residents can achieve home ownership quite cheaply. A true leasehold scheme will provide you with the second best financial outcome when you exit.

Table 9.2 summarises the strengths and weaknesses of the leasehold model.

Table 9.2: leasehold strengths and weaknesses

| Strengths | Weaknesses |
|---|---|
| Low ongoing fees. | Not a common structure. |
| Cheaper buy-in price (typically $200 000–$300 000). | Land is not owned, only the dwelling. |
| Possibility of government allowance for lease component of fees. | Higher ongoing fees due to the lease payments. |

# Company title

Under company title purchase arrangements, a corporation owns the village and a resident buys shares in the company at a value that reflects the property value. Ownership of the shares confers the right to occupy the premises attached to those shares. A board of directors, similar to a residents' committee or owners corporation but with legal powers, is appointed by the shareholders and is responsible for the operation of the village. The corporation and the board of directors are obliged to comply with the company's articles of association and operate within the *Corporations Act* (Commonwealth), as opposed to any state communities titles or residential property legislation.

It is rare to find company title schemes today.

# Rental

Rental is not a purchase arrangement; rather, it describes a scheme under which the owner or operator of a retirement village unit leases the property to you as a tenant. Rental arrangements are governed by your state or territory residential tenancies legislation.

The rent payable under the lease is generally determined by the level of government benefits received by the residents, from programs such as the Age Pension and the Rent Assistance allowance. A typical charge would be 100 per cent of the Rent Assistance allowance and 85 per cent of your pension. This charge may also include linen, laundry and meals.

Rental villages are typically found in fringe and suburban locations and target retirees with limited capital and income. These facilities are generally not registered as retirement villages under the state retirement villages legislation.

The units themselves are usually one-bedroom apartments, often only around 40 square metres in size. They may be furnished or unfurnished and do not include garaged car parking. The complexes offer a central dining facility with meal service; the units themselves have only rudimentary kitchenettes with limited cooking facilities.

In the past, rental villages allowed only tenants to occupy the units; however, many rental villages now allow residents to be owner-occupiers and choose whether they wish to make use of the linen, laundry and meals services. If you do not have the means to buy a retirement unit, then a rental retirement village could be an option for you, as you can buy one of these units for around $120 000 – $150 000.

Be careful, though. I have real concerns about the financial viability of the managers of these villages. While the failure of a village manager should not affect your title to the property in any way, it could make it hard to attract a good manager to the complex. It is also hard to sell out of these units, as there is no established secondary market. Real estate agents are not interested in selling them because of the complexity of the ownership arrangements and the small sales fee involved.

## Deferred management fee

The final and most complex of all purchase arrangements is the deferred management fee or DMF scheme. Most retirement villages in Australia and New Zealand operate under DMF schemes.

DMF schemes have been structured to work within retirement villages legislation, while seeking to meet many Australians' cultural need to own property. This stands in contrast to the retirement living sectors in the US and Europe, where people are much more comfortable with renting.

The DMF scheme is also known as a loan/lease or loan/licence scheme. In essence, an annual fee is incurred by the resident for each year of occupancy, capped at a set number of years, and calculated as a percentage of either the original sale price or the subsequent resale value of the unit.

The original intention of the DMF scheme some 30 years ago was to allow retirees to buy a unit for 20 to 30 per cent less than the market value of an equivalent freehold unit. The village owner would then make that discount back over the next five to ten years through the accrued fee. Unfortunately, today retirement village owners charge residents the full equivalent freehold value of the unit as well as the deferred fee.

The deferred fee is structured around the purchase of a long-term right to occupy contract in the form of a lease or licence (rather than the usual sale of the freehold title) that the resident of an individual unit executes with the village owner. This is a long-term contract between the owner and the resident and commits the latter to paying a management fee that is deferred until such time as the resident vacates the unit. The fee is accrued over the duration of the resident's tenure in the property and is physically received by the operator only upon departure of the resident (the fee is usually retained from the proceeds of the resale).

Under the DMF scheme, residents also pay an ongoing service fee to cover the costs of operating the village, such as insurance, rates, utilities and staffing. The owner of the village contributes to these costs on behalf of the administration areas and any units yet to be sold. Legislation prevents operators from making a profit on service costs so weekly fees are set at the level of actual total costs.

Residents may be offered additional services such as meals, laundry and cleaning. The charge to residents for these services may include a profit component, although this is generally held within a reasonable, commercial range to encourage use of the services by residents. These services may be provided by the owner or outsourced to third parties. Some services may even attract a government subsidy if the resident qualifies for such support.

It is important to reiterate that under a deferred fee scheme the resident does not actually own the freehold title to their unit — this remains with the owner of the village. Instead, the resident purchases a right to occupy, usually in the form of a lease or licence. The resident's occupation right under a deferred fee scheme, however, is similar to freehold title in that it costs residents about the same to acquire it, and they enjoy similar rights of occupation and tenure.

Some freehold retirement villages also charge a deferred fee. In this instance, there is no clear benefit in purchasing a unit in a freehold village and it will not provide you with a better financial outcome when you exit, as outlined earlier in this chapter under the section 'Freehold'. In fact, it can actually work out to be more expensive to purchase owing to the addition of a state stamp duty charge on the purchase price.

Table 9.3 (overleaf) compares the strengths and weaknesses of the DMF model.

Table 9.3: deferred management fee strengths and weaknesses

| Strengths | Weaknesses |
|---|---|
| Usually better complexes with more facilities. | Ongoing liability for resident to fund village fee until unit is sold. |
| Complexes are usually larger. | Freehold title remains with the owner, not the resident. |
| They are better funded and have a range of pricing options. | Owner-operator sustainability risk. |
| Some complexes offer to buy your property if it hasn't sold within an agreed time frame. | Resales typically the responsibility of the owner-manager, whose interests may not be aligned with yours. |
| Owner-manager will typically manage your refurbishment for resale. | Refurbishment obligation on the resident at the end of occupation. |
| Typically owned and operated by larger, more professional organisations. | Ongoing liability to resident from village owner, who may go broke. |
| Most common structure around. | Heavy fee structure. |
| Villa-style houses as well as apartments. | Complex purchase contract. |

# DMF summary

The deferred management fee arrangement is the subject of much angst among retirement community residents. This is not so much because of the unfairness of the contract, but rather because of lack of understanding of how the contract works, which results in unpleasant surprises for residents when they consider moving out.

Deferred fee schemes do weigh heavily in favour of the village owner. Village owners and developers have invested lots of money with accountants and lawyers to design contracts that work within state and federal laws, yet maximise the profit and tax outcomes for the owner. But is this necessarily a bad thing?

Village owners who use deferred fee contracts are not just profit-minded vultures who don't care about their residents. Many not-for-profit operators such as church groups or benevolent organisations also use deferred fee contracts.

Ultimately, successful villages are those with well-funded, engaged owners. The owner that makes a profit from the enterprise will be more inclined to spend money on the maintenance of the community facilities to keep the complex looking fresh and attractive. No-one benefits when a retirement village owner goes broke.

## Chapter summary

- The five different ways that retirees can buy or occupy a home in a retirement village are:
  - strata-title freehold
  - leasehold
  - company title
  - rental
  - the deferred management fee (DMF) scheme.
- Freehold and leasehold schemes that do not apply exit fees deliver the best financial outcomes for residents at exit.
- The DMF scheme is the most common form of contractual arrangement used by retirement villages in Australia. Under a DMF scheme, a village resident accrues a fee for every year in residence. The resident pays this fee on leaving the village when the unit is resold.
- Under deferred fee schemes, a resident may also be obliged to share capital gains with the village operator.

# Chapter 10

## Investing in the retirement living sector

Unless you have been living under a rock for the past ten years you will know that Australia's population, like the rest of the developed world's, is rapidly ageing. The maturing of the country's demographic profile is changing the nature of our living arrangements and driving a boom in the retirement living sector, but is it possible for savvy property investors to get a slice of the action?

The demographic phenomenon is well understood by property companies and investment banks, hence the rapid growth of retirement village ownership by for-profit organisations, as opposed to charities and other not-for-profit operators.

So how can individual investors benefit from this gold rush?

If you don't have enough money to develop your own retirement village as an investment, there are basically two ways that you can get exposure to the sector: indirectly and directly.

### Indirect investment

You can achieve indirect exposure to the retirement living sector simply by investing in companies listed on the ASX that own and operate retirement villages. Table 10.1 (overleaf) shows the large, listed retirement village owners. Outside of owning your own retirement village, buying shares is also the only way that you can invest in retirement villages that use deferred management fee contracts.

All listed retirement village owners are property companies that also have interests in other businesses such as property development and investment. This means you are not getting pure exposure to the retirement living sector, but rather a blended investment in development, retail and commercial assets, as well as retirement villages.

Table 10.1: large, listed retirement village owners

| Company | Size* | Retirement exposure |
|---------|-------|---------------------|
| Lend Lease | $5.0 bn | 70 retirement villages; 32 aged care facilities |
| Stockland Group | $7.5 bn | 61 existing villages, with a substantial development pipeline |
| FKP | $0.75 bn | 76 villages under management, around two-thirds of which are owned by the group |

\* Size relates to the market capitalisation of the company. Market capitalisation is the total dollar value of all the company's shares on offer.

# Direct investment

Rental retirement villages offer one of the only ways for investors to acquire a direct exposure to the retirement sector. As explained in chapter 9, rental retirement villages are communities of units that are purchased by investors specifically for the purpose of renting to retirees.

Rental retirement villages operate under standard residential tenancy agreements. A specialist retirement village management company is appointed by the body corporate or owners corporation to operate the village on behalf of investors. The on-site manager, who is responsible for the day-to-day operation, maintenance and typically the leasing of units to tenants, is an employee of the management company. The management company charges letting and management fees; however, investors are usually free to appoint external real estate agencies for these tasks if they choose. Management companies will typically offer additional services to village residents, such as cleaning and meals, and these services are contracted directly with the tenant.

In the United States most retirement villages operate under a rental model, charging a monthly fee that varies depending on the add-on services used. The rental model for retirement villages is still evolving in Australia. As discussed in chapter 9, this model is generally aimed at the lower socioeconomic demographic. The weekly rent charged has to take account of the Age Pension and Rental Assistance allowances received by retirees, and this may restrict landlords to charging a rent below the market rate for a similar type of property outside of the complex.

Financial planners and property spruikers sold many of these rental retirement complexes to Mum and Dad investors at inflated prices in the 1990s. As a rule, they don't perform well as investments owing to the inability of rents to keep up with the market, and there are concerns about the viability of the business model applied by the management companies. Other owners include developers who have retained stock for letting. The Dutch banking behemoth ING also has a portfolio of rental retirement villages.

## Investment facts

One of the benefits of buying an investment property in a rental village is the low cost of acquisition. It is still possible to buy units for around $100 000, although an average price would be around $140 000–$160 000. However, potential investors should be aware that banks are hesitant to lend against these types of assets.

Investment returns consist of a rental income yield and capital growth over time. You can expect a gross yield of anywhere between 2 and 9 per cent, which is then diluted by the usual property-related expenses such as rates, letting and management fees, and property maintenance.

Because capital gains are constrained by the lack of opportunity for an investor to increase rent, the total value of individual units in the better located villages is likely to be less than the actual value of the land the village occupies!

Unlike normal residential investment property, the performance of a rental village unit will depend largely on the ability of the village manager to attract tenants and increase rent. This adds a layer of management risk to your investment that should be offset by a higher yield or capital growth profile than that of standard residential property investment.

With such a low purchase price, the reluctance of banks to lend against the asset, as well as the constrained yield and capital growth prospects, the logical owners for these properties are owner-occupiers who cannot afford to buy a unit in the more expensive DMF villages. One opportunity for investors is therefore to buy, renovate and on-sell these units to an owner-occupier.

## The resale market

An efficient resale market for these assets does not yet exist. Real estate agents are loath to list them as the low selling price equates to an equally low commission, typically for the same amount of work as a higher priced property. Selling a property for $120000 takes the same time and effort as a property worth three times that amount, so why would they bother?

Consequently, finding units for sale will take investors a little more work. Sometimes units are advertised in the classified sections of seniors' newspapers; however, your best option is to approach the on-site manager of a rental complex and ask if there are any units for sale. You will find that many owners of these units are open to offers whether they are formally for sale or not.

Table 10.2 reviews the strengths and weaknesses of this investment sector.

Table 10.2: strengths and weaknesses of rental village units

| Strengths | Weaknesses |
|---|---|
| Growing demand for them. | They are hard to find. |
| There are few options for retirees to rent. | There is an inefficient secondary resale market. |
| A lack of new supply. | Bigger village manager risk. |
| A lack of low-cost retirement units. | Sub-market rents. |
| Rent may be offset with government rental allowance. | Constrained capital growth prospects. |

Rental units located in retirement villages are currently the average investor's only viable option for direct exposure to the retirement property sector. However, they do pose a significantly higher risk to the investor than standard residential property, so buyers should do careful research and get good advice before proceeding.

## Chapter summary

- The retirement living sector is booming as a result of the country's ageing population. This has attracted investment from property companies and investment banks. However, there are few avenues for the individual investor to gain exposure to this industry.

- Investors can gain indirect exposure to the retirement living sector through buying shares in ASX-listed companies that own retirement villages. These companies include Lend Lease, Stockland and FKP.

- For direct investment, an individual can purchase a unit in a rental retirement village. Rental retirement villages target retirees with a low income and capital base.

- Rental retirement villages are a risky investment and potential buyers should do thorough research and get good advice.

# Analysing your research

Because of the complexity of retirement village purchase contracts and the number of variations between all the different purchase arrangements, it can be very hard to evaluate more than one village and compare apples with apples. In this part of the book I will teach you how to analyse your research and assess the merits of various villages, so you can make a fully informed decision as to which offers you the best deal.

I will start by looking at the various fees and charges you will find in your contract.

# Chapter 11

## Fees and charges

As discussed in chapter 3, living in a retirement village is a great lifestyle choice for retirees. You have to pay for this lifestyle, however, as it brings with it a variety of fees and charges that you would typically not encounter living in your own home.

This chapter outlines the various fees and charges that residents have to pay when they buy, sell or live in a retirement community. You may find that different retirement villages use different names for their fees. You will need to familiarise yourself with the fees explained here and identify the charges as listed in your purchase contract.

Note that although many of the more substantial fees and charges do not become payable until you leave the village, it is important to understand them up-front when you sign the purchase contract so you can gauge the impact they will have on your financial outcome at exit.

I have grouped the fees into three categories to make it easier for you to understand the context of their application and when you can expect to pay them. The three elements are purchasing costs, living costs and exit costs.

## Purchasing costs

Purchasing costs are those costs associated with the purchase of your retirement unit.

## Expression of interest

The first cost you are usually faced with is an expression of interest charge, when you pay the village operator a small sum of money to place a hold on the unit you have selected to buy. It is a small fee of only a couple of hundred dollars and is fully refundable in the event that you decide not to proceed. If you do proceed, the charge is usually put towards your deposit.

## Deposit

Once you have selected a retirement home you will need to hold that property by lodging a deposit with the vendor. The deposit is typically a notional amount of around $1000–$5000, and should be fully refundable in the event that either you or the village operator withdraws from the contract. The deposit amount will come off the sale price of the property when the purchase is settled.

Placing a deposit on a property may not necessarily reserve that property exclusively for you, however. Some operators take several deposits on one property and sell the home to the first buyer who can come up with the cash. Make sure you clearly understand the deposit policy of the village to avoid disappointment.

## Ingoing contribution

A fee unique to the DMF scheme is what is known as an ingoing contribution. This is the amount payable under the contract to secure the right to reside in the retirement village. It is really just a fancy name for the purchase price and is a one-off payment, not a recurrent fee. Interestingly, the ingoing contribution is actually structured as a loan made by you to the village operator, albeit unsecured (except by the licence or loan you have received to occupy your unit) and interest free! It is structured in this way to reduce the operator's taxable income. So don't be confused if when reading your contract you find references to a loan, as this simply refers to your ingoing contribution.

## Contract preparation costs

Another charge at the time of purchase is the apportionment of legal and other expenses incurred by the village owner in the drafting and execution of purchase contracts. Some village operators charge you a contract preparation fee when you first enter the community and then another fee when you leave! This charge is usually around $1000.

# Stamp duty

Stamp duty will usually be applicable to the purchase of freehold title to a piece of land. The village sales agent can advise in the first instance as to what the applicable state calculation is. Double-check this with a solicitor if you are unsure.

# GST

GST is payable on the freehold purchase of newly built dwellings only, although this will simply form part of the purchase price. There is no GST payable on DMF contracts.

## Living costs

The living costs are those fees and charges associated with your stay in the village. These are regular fees charged on a weekly, monthly or quarterly basis.

# Village fee

The village fee is also known as the general services fee or general services charge. This is a regular fee charged to each resident for the funding of costs such as grounds and maintenance, on-site management, insurance and security. Obviously the more services and facilities offered by a village, the higher the charge is likely to be. Conversely, large villages with many units are able to spread the costs over more residents so the fee is likely to be lower.

The village fee is the portion of the annual operating budget for the village that is paid by the occupant of an identified lot, or unit. Lots that are owned by the village operator, such as sales offices, also have an allocated levy which is paid by the village operator. For new complexes, the levies on any units yet to be sold are also covered by the village operator.

Residents, or the retirement community's residents' committee, have varying levels of input and final approval of the budget, and this is outlined in the state's retirement villages legislation and the village rules. By law, no profit component for the village operator should be included in the budget, although this gets messy when the larger village operators levy centralised head office costs, such as management, legal or group insurance contracts, to individual communities within the group. Residents' committees are entitled to ask for a reconciliation of these costs at year-end.

### Sometimes the little guy DOES win ...

ASX-listed retirement village owner-operator Stockland was recently taken to the NSW Consumer, Trader and Tenancy Tribunal by the residents of one of its retirement villages. Among other issues in dispute, Stockland was attempting to include head office charges in the retirement village's annual budget. The residents refused to agree, as they were not sure if the charges were due to work performed by Stockland's head office specifically in the interests of this particular retirement village.

The Tribunal recognised that some functions performed at the head office probably either directly or indirectly provided a service to residents, but that others did not. The Tribunal noted that the lack of information provided by Stockland to the residents during the budget process, and also to the Tribunal, made it impossible to judge which of the functions performed by head office staff could rightly be charged to the village.

The Tribunal found in favour of the residents; however, Stockland is appealing the decision in the NSW District Court.

The village fee is usually charged on a monthly basis. A resident can expect it to increase annually in line with the consumer price index, or as otherwise outlined in the budget, as there may be new or additional costs to be covered in the next budget year.

As a rule of thumb, the fee usually equates to around $100 a week per unit, although it will be higher in villages with more facilities. Leasehold schemes may also have a higher fee as it will include a rent component for the land. As explained in chapter 9, the site rental component of the village fee may attract the Rental Assistance benefit from Centrelink, depending on the eligibility of the resident.

A resident is obliged to continue paying the village fee until such time as the unit is resold. This means that if you move out of your retirement unit, for whatever reason, and it takes six months to resell the unit, you will be obliged to pay the charge over the six months your unit is vacant. Some states have now capped the fee liability time in their retirement villages legislation. This is an entirely reasonable proposition, so if you live in a state or territory that does not cap the duration of the fee liability, you should try to negotiate it into your contract anyway—try for three months, but six months would be an acceptable outcome.

In New South Wales the liability time is capped at six weeks. This means the outgoing resident must continue paying the village fee for up to six weeks after they leave. After six weeks, the fee is split in the same proportion as the sharing of capital gains. More about sharing capital gains shortly.

## Body corporate fee

The owners corporation or body corporate fee is similar to the village fee in what it covers but is associated with strata-titled freehold properties only. The corporation is usually obliged by law to set annual budgets for administration and sinking funds, and there should be a reference to the dollar amount set, such as an independent engineering report. Otherwise the budgets are set annually using the previous year's actual spending amounts with a CPI increase, and the addition of any new spend initiatives.

## Personal services (or services) charge

If a village resident wishes to buy additional services from the operator, such as cleaning, laundry or meals, then the cost for this service is negotiated directly between the resident and the service provider, which could be either the village operator or an external supplier. There may be a contracted time period for the services or a cancellation notice period.

## Exit costs

Exit costs are those charges due and payable when you leave the retirement village.

# Refurbishment costs

Outgoing residents are obliged to fund any necessary refurbishment costs. This is not a fee as such, but rather a contractual obligation for residents to fund the return of their unit to a marketable condition when they leave. A marketable condition means the same general condition as when you first moved in and comparable to other units for sale in the complex. Typically the operator would project manage the refurbishment, but you should take care to agree on the scope and ask for a quote before work commences. Unless it is stipulated in the original purchase contract, residents are under no obligation to use the village operator for this work and can organise it themselves. In practice, however, the village operator would do many of these refurbishments in a year and so could be expected to complete the work in the most time- and cost-effective way.

Retirees are usually gentle on their residences so it is unlikely the cost of any refurbishment will be significant. Typically a fresh coat of paint and new carpet, plus repairing any broken fittings, is all that is needed. An average cost for this work would be around $5000 – $10 000.

There may be a requirement to upgrade the kitchen or bathrooms if the unit was constructed more than 15–20 years ago. This can add significant cost to the refurbishment—perhaps another $5000 for each area. Unless the purchase contract stipulates otherwise, the level of refurbishment should be subject to negotiation between the resident and village operator.

Contracts around the country vary on whether the refurbishment costs are funded by the village owner or the resident. Some states stipulate who should fund the costs in their legislation.

Under some contracts, residents are not released from their contractual obligations until refurbishment and resale of the unit have occurred. This is to protect the owner from vacancies and effectively ensures the complex is potentially able to operate at 100 per cent occupancy. Some village operators buy the unit back themselves or commit to do so if it hasn't sold after an agreed period of time.

A good rule of thumb to use is shown in table 11.1.

Table 11.1: refurbishment costs in the contract

| If... | contract states the resident receives all the capital gain on resale of the unit | then... | resident funds all refurbishment costs. |
|---|---|---|---|
| If... | contract states the resident shares capital gain with village owner on resale of the unit, or the DMF is calculated on the resale price | then... | resident and village owner fund the refurbishment costs in equal proportion to the split of capital gains. |
| If... | contract states the village owner receives all the capital gain on resale of the unit | then... | village owner funds all refurbishment costs. |

## Sales commission or marketing costs

Another fee at exit is the sales commission paid to the selling agent, or the refunding of costs incurred by the village operator in marketing your unit. Larger villages typically have their own sales agents located in a sales office on site. However, unless their contract states otherwise, residents should be free to appoint any agent to sell the unit or even to do it themselves. I recommend you make use of the on-site sales agent, who is best placed to sell the unit. Your average real estate sales agent based outside the complex will probably struggle to understand the purchase contract, let alone explain it to prospective purchasers.

In Queensland, sales commissions on freehold properties are capped at 5 per cent for the first $18 000, then 2.5 per cent on the balance of the sale price, although you can negotiate a lower fee than this. Other states and territories do not regulate sales commissions, which can be negotiated directly with your selling agent.

For deferred fee schemes in most states the resident and village operator must agree in writing on the sale price. If they are unable to agree, an independent valuation must be commissioned and the resulting valuation used to determine the sale price. Understandably, the cost of this valuation should be split equally between the village operator and the outgoing resident, but some villages may try to charge you for the full amount of the valuation.

## Deferred management (or exit) fee

When I first came across the deferred fee scheme while working for a retirement village owner, I couldn't believe it was legal! In a good retirement village this scheme can in effect be a licence to print money.

This is how it works. A village owner will develop a site and sell occupancy licences or leases to residents for a price equivalent to the freehold value of a normal residential unit of similar size and standard. This first sale presents the owner with its first windfall — the development margin. The development margin is the profit made on the first sale of a unit and represents the difference between the cost of building the unit and the sale price. Development margins are usually in the range of 20 to 25 per cent, so if you buy a unit for $100 000, around $25 000 of your purchase price is profit for the village owner.

The resident then pays a weekly fee that covers all the running costs for the village, including management expenses, thereby eliminating virtually all holding costs for the village owner (assuming the village is 100 per cent occupied).

When the residents depart the village, they pay to the owner the deferred management fee they have accrued for every year they were in residence. In addition, any capital growth that is realised on resale is likely to be shared with the owner. There may also be a sales commission or marketing expenses of up to 3 per cent of the resale price.

With this model, a village owner is able to discount initial sales quite heavily and sacrifice some of its development margin, in the knowledge that it will make it back on the next resale of the unit. Compare this with a residential property developer who gets only one shot at selling a unit and crystallising its development margin;

any discount on sales price in that case comes off the development margin and is gone forever.

So the retirement village owner not only gets the development margin when a unit is first sold, but it also retains an interest in every sale that occurs thereafter, providing it with an income stream in perpetuity. This is an unbelievably good financial arrangement for the village owner, but the cash flows can be quite volatile. There may be many resales one year but none the next. To own villages that operate with deferred fee schemes, a company needs to have a strong balance sheet (low debt) and cash flow from other sources to fund it during the lean times.

Key variables that can affect investment returns for village owners include sale price, how quickly the sale is made, the length of time it takes to settle a transaction and the average length of tenure for residents in the village.

Now this raises an important point for you to note: the average length of tenure for a resident in a village is around 10 years, or at least that's the figure independent valuers use when valuing these properties. So if a village owner realises income only when a resident departs and resells the unit, the owner is making money out of only 10 per cent of the village inventory each year. If the average length of tenure is lower, then more units are sold each year and the village owner makes more money faster.

So how do village owners influence or reduce the average length of tenure to encourage faster exits? Simple: they try to increase the average age of their village residents by encouraging older purchasers. Logically, the older unit purchasers are, the shorter their residence is likely to be. If you are on the younger side of retirement you may find a less than enthusiastic welcome at some villages that are trying to increase the average age of their residents. Conversely, retirement home buyers aged 80 or more are welcomed with open arms!

The deferred management fee, also known as the exit or departure fee, is found in loan/lease or loan/licence contracts, as well as some freehold contracts. As mentioned previously, the DMF is an annual fee charged for each year of occupancy, capped at a set number of years, and calculated as a percentage of either the original purchase price or the subsequent resale value of the lease or licence. The fee is accrued annually at each anniversary of the resident's commencement at the village, and paid out to the village owner from the proceeds of the resale of the unit. The fee varies between villages, within villages and also between states.

An example of a typical DMF contract is shown in table 11.2.

Table 11.2: a sample DMF contract

|  | Year 1 | Year 2 | Year 3 | Year 4 | Year 5 | – | Year 10 |
|---|---|---|---|---|---|---|---|
| Annual (%) | 2.5 | 2.5 | 2.5 | 2.5 | 2.5 | – | 2.5 |
| Cumulative (%) | 2.5 | 5.0 | 7.5 | 10.0 | 12.5 | – | 25.0 |

In this example I use a contract known as a 25 over 10—that is, a 25 per cent deferred management fee accrued over 10 years.

I assume that the fee is spread equally over the 10-year period, therefore 2.5 per cent is accrued each year, and after 10 years a total fee of 25 per cent has been accrued. This is just an example, however, and total fees can range anywhere from 20 per cent to 40 per cent or more.

Under a DMF scheme a resident is free to vacate the unit at any time, but is liable for the accumulated portion of the fee if the departure occurs before the capped fee year. In this example, a resident who departed in year five would be liable for the fee accrued to date of 12.5 per cent; for the resident who left in year 12, the obligation would remain at the capped amount of 25 per cent.

Some villages, particularly those where the residents stay for only a short time, front-load the bulk of the fee into the first few years of a resident's occupancy, instead of averaging the fee equally over the accrual period. Under a 25 over 10 structure, a village operator might make the first year 8 per cent, the second 5 per cent and every year thereafter 1.5 per cent. This ensures that a resident in occupation for only three or so years ends up paying the majority of the deferred management fee.

Table 11.3 sets out an actual calculation of this fee, using the assumptions of a 25 over 10 contract.

Table 11.3: a sample DMF 25 over 10 contract calculation

| | |
|---|---|
| Initial unit purchase price | $450 000 |
| Assumed exit | End of year 10 |
| Unit resale price | $750 000 |
| Share of capital gain with operator | 50/50 |
| **At exit:** | |
| Deferred fee payable (25% of entry price) | $112 500 |
| Share of capital gain to village owner (50%) | $150 000 |
| **Total return to the resident** | **$487 500** |
| **Total return to the village owner** | **$262 500** |

In this example the resident purchases a unit for $450 000. After 10 years of occupation the resident exits and sells the unit for $750 000. Under this contract the seller is obliged to split the capital gains on exit equally with the owner. (I will discuss this in more detail shortly.)

At exit, the deferred fee component payable, calculated at 25 per cent of the entry price, is $112 500. The capital gain of $300 000 is shared equally between the resident and operator and amounts to $150 000 each. So the total return to the resident is $487 500, and the total return to the village operator is $262 500.

Note that the resident has only just broken even after 10 years of capital growth, although this doesn't include other expenses such as sales commissions or marketing costs.

Retirement village sales agents will usually explain this away by arguing that this purchase is a lifestyle decision and not an investment. In a way, they are right: you are no longer at the asset accumulation stage of your life, and now is the right time to be spending the fruits of your labours over the past 50 or 60 years. However, I see no reason not to apply the same level of financial analysis and due diligence to this purchase as if the seller was 30 years younger.

## Share of capital gain on sale

Under deferred management fee purchase contracts, residents may be obliged to share any capital gains with the village owner on the resale of their unit, or even entirely forfeit them. Generally, if the fee is calculated on the exit price, there should be limited or no capital gains payable. If it is calculated on the purchase price, the resident gets the benefit of knowing what the fee will be up front, but will likely have to share any capital gains made on resale with the owner. Most contracts contain a 50/50 split of capital gains, although some owners have been known to take 100 per cent. Just to be clear, this is in addition to the deferred management fee. However, there are no laws governing this and village operators are free to choose whichever structure they prefer.

Capital gains are realised when a resident leaves and the unit is resold. Upon resale, the village owner returns the sale proceeds to the previous resident after subtracting the deferred management fee and the village owner's contracted share of the capital gain. The return of these sales proceeds after the removal of all fees and charges is known in some contracts as the exit entitlement.

As you would expect, if you resell your unit for less than your original purchase price, then you wear the entirety of the loss. Some purchase contracts also oblige a departing resident to make up any loss to the village owner in the event that the unit sells for less than the resident initially paid. For example, if you bought your unit for $100 000 and resold it for $80 000, then you would have to make up the $20 000 loss to the village owner.

I have seen some contracts in which, instead of using a fixed percentage share of the capital gains, the sharing of capital gains is scaled according to the deferred management fee.

Table 11.4 gives an example of this.

Table 11.4: scaling the share of capital gains

|  | Year 1 | Year 2 | Year 3 | Year 4 | Year 5 | – | Year 10 |
|---|---|---|---|---|---|---|---|
| DMF annual (%) | 2.5 | 2.5 | 2.5 | 2.5 | 2.5 | – | 2.5 |
| DMF cumulative (%) | 2.5 | 5.0 | 7.5 | 10.0 | 12.5 | – | 25.0 |
| Share of gain (%) | 2.5 | 5.0 | 7.5 | 10.0 | 12.5 | – | 25.0 |

In this table the share of capital gain mirrors the cumulative deferred fee charged: in year one the village operator would receive 2.5 per cent of any gains; in year 10 it would receive 25 per cent of any gains.

### Industry average statistics

As mentioned in chapter 10, one of the largest retirement village owner-operators in Australia is the FKP Group, an ASX-listed property developer that owns or manages around 76 retirement villages. With such a large chunk of the market under its control, we can look at some of the statistics across its portfolio, as we do in table 11.5, to get a feel for the average fees and charges applied across the retirement living industry.

Table 11.5: FKP portfolio statistics

| Key indicator | Result |
|---|---|
| Average turnover (tenure) | 9 years |
| Average DMF and capital gain per transaction | $88 000 |
| Average DMF | 30% |
| Average share of capital gains | 51% |
| Average age of residents | 82.2 years |

From this table, when you start your research you could expect to find the average DMF across the industry at around 30 per cent and the sharing of capital gains at around 50 per cent. Use this as your benchmark—anything lower could be good value; anything higher is out of line with the industry average and probably overpriced.

## Maintenance reserve fund

Some retirement village purchase contracts oblige the departing resident to pay a percentage of their original ingoing contribution or purchase price, usually around 2–3 per cent, into a maintenance reserve fund. This is not an additional fee payable to the village owner, as they are obliged to forward this payment into the village maintenance reserve fund. The fund is like a kitty that all departing residents contribute to. It is used to fund the major refurbishment or upgrade works of the common areas, and is an additional cost to you when departing the village.

## Chapter summary

The fees and charges associated with living in a retirement community include:

- Purchasing costs:
    - expression of interest fee
    - deposit
    - ingoing contribution
    - contract preparation costs
    - stamp duty
    - GST.
- Living costs:
    - village fee or general services charge
    - personal services charge
    - body corporate or owners corporation fee.
- Exit costs:
    - refurbishment costs
    - sales commission or marketing costs
    - deferred management fee
    - sharing of capital gains
    - maintenance reserve fund.

# Chapter 12

## Analysis and evaluation

Let's start this chapter by recapping where you should be now with your planning.

Have you...

- planned your retirement lifestyle?
- decided to move into a retirement village?
- completed the preference questionnaire?
- chosen a location (where to retire)?
- chosen the type of unit to buy—an apartment or a villa?
- understood the purchase arrangements?
- understood how the fees and charges work?
- compiled a list of villages in your chosen location?
- researched your list using the individual village questionnaire?
- summarised your research onto the research comparison worksheet?

If you have checked off all these questions, then it is now time to analyse and evaluate your research material. Your research data should consist of the completed individual village questionnaires and research comparison worksheet along with any supporting brochures or documentation.

By this stage you have probably pretty much decided which village on your shortlist you prefer. Now we will see if we can analyse your research material to support that preference, or perhaps to demonstrate a better option for you.

# Analysing the purchase price

The very first problem you will face is the asking price. How can you tell if this price is reasonable or inflated or actually represents a good buy?

Prices of retirement village units typically mirror those in the surrounding residential property sector, so initially the best way to assess the reasonableness of the asking price is to compare it with similar properties in the neighbouring suburbs. The best and easiest way to do this is to arrive at a cost per square metre for the properties to be compared.

You derive a price per square metre by dividing the asking or sale price of a property by the total square metres of the internal built area. As an example, table 12.1 compares the prices of four retirement village units, labelled A–D.

Table 12.1: comparing price per square metre

|  | A | B | C | D |
|---|---|---|---|---|
| Asking price | $400 000 | $485 000 | $425 000 | $410 000 |
| Size (sq. m.) | 100 | 135 | 110 | 120 |
| Price per sq. m. | $4000 | $3593 | $3864 | $3417 |
| Average price per sq. m. | $3699 | | | |
| Deviation from the average | 8% | –3% | 4% | –8% |

On the top line you can see the asking prices of the different units, and on the next line the internal size of each unit. Divide the asking price by the internal size to come up with the price per square metre, which you can see calculated for you on the next line. Next you find the average price per square metre of all the units by dividing the total of all the asking prices by the total of all the internal areas. The deviation from the average is the percentage difference between each unit's price per square metre and the average price.

When you compare the price per square metre for each unit with the average for the group, you can see that property A is 8 per cent higher than the average, property B is 3 per cent below, property C is 4 per cent higher and property D is 8 per cent lower.

On the face of it, then, property D, with an asking price that is 8 per cent lower than the average, looks to be the best buy. However, using this data as a starting point, you would then consider each property in light of its less quantitative features, such as land size, views, standard of finishes and location. In this instance, for example, property A may be two blocks walk from the beach, whereas property D may be located on a busy road.

The total square metres of a unit considers internal floor space only and should not include areas such as balconies, pergolas, garages and decking. This is because these areas typically cost less than the internal built area and can vary greatly in size. So it is best not to include these areas, but if you do, then make sure you are consistent and include them in each comparison property price per square metre calculation.

Most retirement village sales brochures feature floor plans with the size of each area clearly identified. For comparable local residential properties, simply scan the existing list of properties for sale in the same area in the paper or on the internet, or speak with local real estate agents. A good way to find local sales data is to purchase a report listing the sales in the area over the past 12 or 24 months from My RP Data <www.myrpdata.com.au>, Residex <www.residex. com.au> or Australian Property Monitors <www.homepriceguide. com.au>. Alternatively, use the website On the House <www. onthehouse.com.au> to find past sales data. Sales of retirement village units will not show up on these reports, as they are not considered to be freehold sales.

The price per square metre calculation does not include land area, so if you are comparing detached or semi-detached retirement houses or villas, then remember to include the size of the land area in your considerations, although not in your calculations. If you examined two directly comparable units, one of which had a larger land plot, the unit with the larger land plot should have a higher purchase price to take into account the larger land size.

The price per square metre calculation for all your comparison properties should be roughly similar. Variances can usually be attributed to variations in the quality of the finishes, the age of the building, the location or whether the unit has views/perspectives. Directly comparable properties (those of equivalent age, standard and condition) should be much the same price. This provides you with a good indication of the benchmark price for a particular style of property in a particular area, and a good base from which to start your price negotiations with the vendor.

Some retirement village operators claim that village units cost around 80 to 85 per cent of comparable residential properties. In my experience, however, retirement village units are typically equivalent in price or even higher than comparable properties in the same area.

## Analysing your DMF contract

As discussed in chapter 9, deferred management fee contracts are complex and confusing. In this section I will show you some of the variations of the contractual arrangements and the impact they have on your financial outcome when you exit.

## DMF review

To recap, the DMF scheme, also known as a loan/lease or loan/licence scheme, entails an annual fee charged to the resident for each year of occupancy, capped at a set number of years and calculated as a percentage of either the original sale price or the subsequent resale value of the licence.

The deferred fee is structured around a long-term right to occupy contract in the form of a lease or licence, which the resident of an individual unit executes with the village owner. The contract commits the resident to paying a management fee that is deferred until such time as the resident vacates the unit. The fee is accrued over the duration of the resident's tenure in the property and is physically received by the operator only upon departure of the resident and the resale of the retirement unit.

Under the DMF scheme, residents pay a weekly service fee (the village fee) to the owner to cover the costs of operating the village, such as insurance, rates, utilities and staffing. The owner of the village also contributes to these costs on behalf of the areas they own and any units yet to be sold.

Under most deferred fee schemes, the resident does not actually own the freehold title to the unit—this remains with the owner of the village.

# Key DMF contract variables

When you get closer to making a decision on a preferred retirement community, the village operator is obliged to provide you with a disclosure statement that outlines the various fees and charges associated with living in the village. For deferred fee contracts, there are certain key terms and conditions that you need to pick out of the wording to assist with your financial analysis of the purchase.

The key variables are as follows:

- *Calculation base.* The calculation base refers to whether the deferred fee is based on the ingoing contribution (the purchase or entry price) or the resale price (the exit price).

- *The actual deferred fee amount.* The actual deferred fee amount is the total deferred fee charged to the resident and ranges anywhere from 10 per cent to around 40 per cent of the original entry price or the exit price of the unit.

- *The years charged.* This number represents the total number of years over which the deferred fee amount is charged.

- *The percentage charge incurred each year.* This is the actual percentage of the deferred fee charged for every year of a resident's occupation. The percentage charged may be the same each year. However, it has become a recent trend, particularly in those villages with a short average length of tenure, to front-load the fee into the first few years of occupation.

- *The share of the capital gain.* If the deferred fee is calculated on the ingoing contribution or original purchase price, then it is typical for any capital gain realised on resale of the unit to be split with the village owner. The share of the gain in this context is the proportion of the capital gain payable to the village owner. Most purchase contracts lock in a set percentage amount payable to the village owner; however, some villages track the share of capital gain to the deferred fee amount. For example, if the deferred fee had accrued to 9 per cent after three years of occupation, then the village operator's share of the capital gain (if any) would also be 9 per cent.

Be wary of operators that boast of a contract under which the resident receives all the capital gain: often these contracts are simply arrangements by which the deferred fee is calculated on the exit price, with no apportionment of capital gains to the village operator. In this case, the operator is still getting exposure to the capital gain through the deferred fee calculated on the exit price—it is really just smoke and mirrors!

There are other factors that can influence your financial outcome at exit but may not necessarily be part of the contract:

- *Village fee or general services charge.* As discussed in chapters 5 and 11, the village fee is the regular, ongoing fee, paid by a resident on a weekly, fortnightly, monthly or quarterly basis, that covers village expenses such as insurance, maintenance, management and security. A resident is obliged to keep paying this fee after exit until their unit is resold. Some states now cap the time the fee must be paid after exit to around 90 days. After this time there may be an apportionment of this fee along the same lines as the sharing of capital gains.

- *Sales commission or marketing costs.* Sales commission is the fee charged to a departing resident for selling the unit. It may be charged as a flat fee but is typically a percentage of the sale price. Instead of charging a sales commission, some village operators charge the outgoing resident for marketing costs associated with the sale of the unit.

- *Stamp duty.* Depending on state regulations, stamp duty may be applicable on a retirement home purchase. Typically this is for freehold properties that include a land component.

- *Capital growth.* Capital growth refers to the increase in the value of the property over time. A capital gain is realised if a unit is sold for more than the original purchase price.

# Examples of key contract variables

The best way to appreciate the impact some of the key contract variables can have on your financial outcome at exit is to run variations of the terms through a 10–year forecast.

## Example 1

In the first example we will use base contract terms of a 25 over 10 contract, which is a 25 per cent fee calculated over 10 years and capped at the end of year 10. This equates to 2.5 per cent every year for 10 years. The fee calculation is based on the ingoing contribution, with any capital gain realised upon resale split equally between the resident and village operator. For this example we will estimate the annual capital growth rate at 4.5 per cent.

Let's assume that the resident has purchased a unit for $450000. At an annual average capital growth rate of 4.5 per cent, the property grows in value until the resident exits at the end of year 10 and resells the unit for $699000. The relevant calculations are set out in table 12.2.

Table 12.2: a sample DMF contract based on 25 over 10 (entry)

**Key contract variables**

| | |
|---|---|
| Deferred fee | 25% |
| Fee calculation | Entry |
| Years charged | 10 |
| DMF per year | 2.50% |
| Share of capital gain | 50/50 |
| Capital growth | 4.50% |

**Ten year forecast ($'000)**

| | Yr 1 | Yr 2 | Yr 3 | Yr 4 | Yr 5 | Yr 6 | Yr 7 | Yr 8 | Yr 9 | Yr 10 |
|---|---|---|---|---|---|---|---|---|---|---|
| A Purchase price −$450 | | | | | | | | | | |
| B Property/Sale value | $470 | $491 | $514 | $537 | $561 | $586 | $612 | $640 | $669 | $699 |
| C DMF % | 2.5% | 5.0% | 7.5% | 10.0% | 12.5% | 15.0% | 17.5% | 20.0% | 22.5% | 25.0% |
| D DMF $ | −11 | −23 | −34 | −45 | −56 | −68 | −79 | −90 | −101 | −113 |
| E Share of gain | −10 | −21 | −32 | −44 | −56 | −68 | −81 | −95 | −110 | −125 |
| F **Net return on exit** | $449 | $448 | $448 | $449 | $449 | $451 | $452 | $455 | $458 | $462 |
| G **Profit/(loss)** | −$1 | −$2 | −$2 | −$2 | −$1 | $1 | $2 | $5 | $8 | $12 |

The allocation of the deferred fee equally across 10 years is shown in row C, 'DMF %', and equates to 2.5 per cent per year, with the total fee of 25 per cent achieved only at the end of year 10. The applicable dollar amounts incurred at the end of each year are shown immediately below in row D, 'DMF $'.

Remember also that any capital gains achieved on the resale of the unit are split equally with the village operator, so the calculation of the share of the gain paid to the operator is shown in row E, 'Share of gain'.

The 'Net return on exit' shown in row F is the resident's exit entitlement—that is, the share of the resale proceeds following the removal of the deferred fee and the village operator's share of the capital gain. In this example, the resident's exit entitlement at the end of year 10 is $462 000, showing a gain of $12 000 over their original purchase price. Note that the resident does not recoup the original ingoing contribution until year six, although the whole arrangement is pretty much even across the first nine years. This particular contract is not a bad outcome for the resident, who by the end of year 10 has actually paid nothing to live in the village, save for the regular village fee, which would have been similar to the holding costs of a freehold property anyway.

After year 10 the fee is capped in this example, so any capital growth achieved after this time will have a significantly positive impact on the resident's financial outcome. This is why planning to stay in a retirement village for the long term and finding a community with good capital growth prospects are so important to your financial outcome when you leave.

Let's now take a look at some variations of the key contract terms and the effect they have on the financial outcome for the resident.

## Example 2

For our first variation we will change the deferred fee amount—let's use instead a fee of 30 per cent, an increase of just 5 per cent over the previous example. Now follow the calculations in table 12.3.

Table 12.3: a sample DMF contract based on 30 over 10 (entry)

**Key contract variables**

| | |
|---|---|
| Deferred fee | 30% |
| Fee calculation | Entry |
| Years charged | 10 |
| DMF per year | 3.00% |
| Share of capital gain | 50/50 |
| Capital Growth | 4.50% |

**Ten year forecast ($'000)**

| | Yr 1 | Yr 2 | Yr 3 | Yr 4 | Yr 5 | Yr 6 | Yr 7 | Yr 8 | Yr 9 | Yr 10 |
|---|---|---|---|---|---|---|---|---|---|---|
| A Purchase price –$450 | | | | | | | | | | |
| B Property/Sale value | $470 | $491 | $514 | $537 | $561 | $586 | $612 | $640 | $669 | $699 |
| C DMF % | 3.0% | 6.0% | 9.0% | 12.0% | 15.0% | 18.0% | 21.0% | 24.0% | 27.0% | 30.0% |
| D DMF $ | –14 | –27 | –41 | –54 | –68 | –81 | –95 | –108 | –122 | –135 |
| E Share of gain | –10 | –21 | –32 | –44 | –56 | –68 | –81 | –95 | –110 | –125 |
| F Net return on exit | $447 | $444 | $442 | $440 | $438 | $437 | $437 | $437 | $438 | $440 |
| G Profit/(loss) | –$4 | –$7 | –$9 | –$11 | –$12 | –$13 | –$14 | –$13 | –$12 | –$11 |

With a 30 per cent fee, the contract results in a loss at exit if the resident leaves the village at any time within 10 years; however, the loss amount is not high. Table 12.3 shows a loss of $11 000 after 10 years in row G, which is actually a pretty good outcome as the original investment amount is still largely intact.

The key point to note, however, is that this outcome depends on annual capital growth of at least 4.5 per cent.

## Example 3

For example 3 we will again use a 30 per cent deferred fee, only this time we will calculate the fee on the exit or resale price, as opposed to the entry price. Table 12.4 outlines the calculations.

Table 12.4: a sample DMF contract based on 30 over 10 (exit)

**Key contract variables**

| | |
|---|---|
| Deferred fee | 30% |
| Fee calculation | Exit |
| Years charged | 10 |
| DMF per year | 3.00% |
| Share of capital gain | 0 |
| Capital growth | 4.50% |

**Ten year forecast ($'000)**

| | Yr 1 | Yr 2 | Yr 3 | Yr 4 | Yr 5 | Yr 6 | Yr 7 | Yr 8 | Yr 9 | Yr 10 |
|---|---|---|---|---|---|---|---|---|---|---|
| A Purchase price −$450 | | | | | | | | | | |
| B Property/sale value | $470 | $491 | $514 | $537 | $561 | $586 | $612 | $640 | $669 | $699 |
| C DMF % | 3.0% | 6.0% | 9.0% | 12.0% | 15.0% | 18.0% | 21.0% | 24.0% | 27.0% | 30.0% |
| D DMF $ | −14 | −29 | −46 | −64 | −84 | −105 | −129 | −154 | −181 | −210 |
| E Share of gain | 0 | 0 | 0 | 0 | 0 | 0 | 0 | 0 | 0 | 0 |
| F Net return on exit | $456 | $462 | $468 | $473 | $477 | $481 | $483 | $486 | $488 | $489 |
| G Profit/(loss) | $6 | $12 | $18 | $23 | $27 | $31 | $33 | $36 | $38 | $39 |

Because the 30 per cent deferred fee calculation in this example is based on the exit price, there is no sharing of the capital gain with the village operator as the exit-based fee already includes an exposure to capital growth. As you can see in row G, this arrangement results in a far superior outcome for the resident, who breaks even from year one. This is because the deferred fee of 3 per cent charged each year is not as high as the annual capital growth of the property at 4.5 per cent.

The results of the contract derivations are compared in table 12.5.

Table 12.5: summary of DMF contract variation

|  | Ex. 1 | Ex. 2 | Ex. 3 | Ex. 4 |
|---|---|---|---|---|
| Deferred fee (%) | 25 | 30 | 30 | 25 |
| Fee calculation | Entry | Entry | Exit | Exit |
| Years | 10 | 10 | 10 | 10 |
| Share of capital gain (%) | 50 | 50 | n/a | n/a |
| Share of capital gain ($'000) | $124 | $124 | n/a | n/a |
| Deferred fee ($) | 113k | 135k | 210 | 175 |
| Resident net return ($'000) | $462 | $439 | $489 | $524 |
| Gain/(loss) by year 10 ($'000) | $12 | ($11) | $39 | $74 |

In example 1 we used the base contract of 25 per cent over 10 years, with a 50/50 split of the capital gain and the fee calculation based on the entry price. This allowed the resident to pretty much break even after 10 years.

In example 2 we tried the same contract, but with a 30 per cent deferred fee. This resulted in a minor loss of $11 000 after 10 years of occupation.

In example 3 we looked at the same 30 per cent over 10 years contract using an exit price-based fee, with the resident taking all of the capital gains. On the table, as example 4, you can also see a 25 per cent over 10 years contract using an exit price-based fee for comparison purposes. It is clear from this table that an exit-based fee works in your favour, because after 10 years you not only preserve your original investment but also achieve a modest profit.

Despite this analysis, it is worth highlighting once again that you are not evaluating an investment here — that is, you are not trying to determine the best return for your money. Rather, you are trying to find a contract that will allow you to keep the majority of your original investment intact.

## Front-loading the deferred fee

I mentioned earlier that when retirement villages have a short average length of stay, the operator front-loads the fee into the first few years, rather than spreading it across a longer period of time such as 10 years. Remember also that the average length of stay used by retirement village valuers is 10 years, which is why we are using a 10-year model here to assess the contract variations.

## Example 4

Let's take a look now at the impact of a front-loaded fee using our original example 1 contract of 25 over 10, based on the entry price, with an equal sharing of capital gains on exit. Table 12.6 outlines the calculations.

Table 12.6: a sample DMF contract with front-loaded fee

**Key contract variables**

| Deferred fee | 25% |
| Fee calculation | Entry |
| Years charged | 4 |
| DMF per year | ? |
| Share of capital gain | 50/50 |
| Capital growth | 4.50% |

**Ten year forecast ('000)**

| | Yr 1 | Yr 2 | Yr 3 | Yr 4 | Yr 5 | Yr 6 | Yr 7 | Yr 8 | Yr 9 | Yr 10 |
|---|---|---|---|---|---|---|---|---|---|---|
| A Purchase price −$450 | | | | | | | | | | |
| B Property/sale value | $470 | $491 | $514 | $537 | $561 | $586 | $612 | $640 | $669 | $699 |
| C DMF % | 10.0% | 17.0% | 22.0% | 25.0% | 25.0% | 25.0% | 25.0% | 25.0% | 25.0% | 25.0% |
| D DMF $ | −45 | −77 | −99 | −113 | −113 | −113 | −113 | −113 | −113 | −113 |
| E Share of gain | −10 | −21 | −32 | −44 | −56 | −68 | −81 | −95 | −110 | −125 |
| F Net return on exit | $415 | $394 | $383 | $381 | $393 | $406 | $419 | $433 | $447 | $462 |
| G Profit/(loss) | −$35 | −$56 | −$67 | −$69 | −$57 | −$45 | −$32 | −$18 | −$3 | $12 |

Instead of spreading the fee evenly across 10 years like the 25 over 10 contract, the deferred fee is front-loaded into the first four years — 10 per cent in the first year, 7 per cent in the second,

5 per cent in the third and 3 per cent in the fourth year. This 25 over 4 contract arrangement puts the resident at a loss right from the start, with break-even occurring only in the final year. You can see here that an exit in year four would be devastating, taking out a quarter of the resident's original investment as the deferred fee.

Interestingly, the result at the end of year 10 is exactly the same for the village operator and the resident, whether the fee is front-loaded or spread evenly. What this tactic does, however, is punish a resident for leaving the village early.

## The impact of capital growth

In all the previous examples we used an annual capital growth rate of 4.5 per cent. A better growth rate will give you a better outcome at exit, whereas a lower growth rate will result in a worse outcome. Capital growth is integral to the quality of your financial outcome at exit.

In fact, capital growth is so important that I have dedicated a whole chapter to the subject! Chapter 13 will explain what capital growth is, what influences the capital growth of retirement villages and finally how to estimate the capital growth prospects for particular suburbs. Table 13.1 on p. 124 summarises a variety of capital growth scenarios under a DMF contract to show you the impact on the financial outcome at exit.

## Comparing different contracts

One of the biggest problems when analysing more than one retirement village is the sheer variety of different purchase prices, contracts, fees and charges, which can make it difficult for you as a potential purchaser to easily compare apples with apples and figure out which retirement village offers the best deal. Along with the purchase price, you need to take into account the village fees, deferred fees, any sharing of capital gains, refurbishment arrangements and, of course, capital growth prospects.

***Contract Comparison Calculator***

To simplify your assessment of the purchase contracts of more than one retirement village, I have designed an online calculator that compares the key contract terms and shows what each village will cost you when you leave (the calculator is similar to the mortgage calculators you find on bank websites). You can access this calculator on our website by simply logging on to <www.findmyretirementhome.com.au> and signing in to the members' section using the password noted in the introduction to this book.

To use the calculator, you will need all the data you have gathered in the individual village questionnaires and summarised in the research comparison worksheet. On the website there is a video tutorial instructing you how to use the calculator, as well as detailed written instructions.

Each of the different purchase arrangements—freehold, leasehold and deferred management fee—has its own unique range of fees and charges that you must take into account when comparing one village purchase with another. The best way to compare options across different purchase arrangements is to order the costs into three categories (as described in chapter 11 and further defined in table 12.7):

- Purchase costs—one-off costs associated with the purchase
- Living costs—the regular weekly or monthly fees associated with living in the village
- Exit costs—the fees and charges incurred when you leave the property.

Table 12.7: fee identification summary

|              | Freehold        | Leasehold       | DMF                        |
|--------------|-----------------|-----------------|----------------------------|
| **At purchase** | deposit         | deposit         | deposit ingoing            |
|              | purchase price  | purchase price  | contribution               |
| **Living costs** | owners corp. fees | owners corp. fees | oillage fees            |
|              |                 | site rental     |                            |

|  | **Freehold** | **Leasehold** | **DMF** |
|---|---|---|---|
| **Exit costs** | sales commission | sales commission | sales commission or marketing costs |
|  | contract prep. costs | contract prep. costs | contract prep. costs |
|  |  |  | share of capital gains |
|  |  |  | refurbishment |
|  |  |  | deferred fee |
|  |  |  | maintenance reserve fund |

Now you can begin your analysis by following these steps:

- *Step 1.* Total the purchase costs associated with each property.

- *Step 2.* Find a total for the living costs associated with each property over the same period of time. I suggest you use a five-year period and a 10-year period. For example, if one of your prospective purchases charges a village fee of $480 per month, you would calculate this as an annual amount ($480 × 12 months = $5760) and then multiply the annual amount by five to arrive at the five-year total ($5760 × 5 years = $28 800), and multiply by 2 to get the 10-year amount ($5760 × 10 years = $57 600).

- *Step 3.* Estimate a selling price for each property, assuming a sale at the end of year five and year 10. Use the directions in chapter 13 to assist in making an educated guess as to the likely growth of your property over five and 10 years.

- *Step 4.* Find a total for the exit costs associated with each property, assuming an exit in year five and year 10. You will need to use your estimated selling price from step 3, as many of the exit costs are calculated as a proportion of this amount (i.e. the sales commission and deferred fee).

- *Step 5.* Finally, use table 12.8 (overleaf) for each village to find the best purchase arrangement.

Table 12.8: fee comparison

| | Year 5 | Year 10 | Example (Year 10) |
|---|---|---|---|
| Purchase costs | ............ | ............ | –$450 000 |
| Living costs | ............ | ............ | –$57 600 |
| Exit costs | ............ | ............ | –$267 000 |
| Resale price | ............ | ............ | $699 000 |
| **Total** | ............ | ............ | –$75 600 |

The figure shown in the last row is the total cost of a property over the period you live in it, including the purchasing costs, the ongoing holding costs, such as the village fee, and the fees involved in selling the property. It is also the figure you use to compare one property or purchase contract with another. (It does not include contents insurance, as this cost should not vary dramatically between villages; however, you could always add it in if differences in insurance quotes for each location are substantial.)

The benefit of using this analysis is that it distils each of your village purchase options down to a single figure that captures all the fees and charges as well as the capital growth potential of each site: the village featuring the lowest loss or the highest total amount is the best financial option. Using both a five- and a 10-year exit assumption takes into account those villages that may have front-loaded their fee, as these properties will show a very bad outcome in year five, but may have caught up to the comparison properties by year 10.

Our modelling shows that DMF contracts featuring a 25 per cent fee apportioned equally over 10 years start to break even in about year eight of a contract (assuming annual capital growth of around 4 to 5 per cent).

### Analysis tip

Your goal should be to find a purchase contract through which you will recoup your ingoing contribution if you leave the village within 10 years. Typically this will not occur until year nine or ten. Any contract that shows a negative return beyond 10 years, I believe, is too much in favour of the retirement village operator.

Use this analysis to negotiate your contract. Your objective will be to get to that break-even point at which you recoup your ingoing contribution as early in your tenure as possible. Your analysis can be tweaked to take account of the different contract scenarios you might negotiate, such as a lower purchase price but higher DMF, or a higher purchase price and lower share of capital gain going to the village owner.

You are always better off getting your discount up front on the purchase price, rather than at the back end with, say, a lower exit fee. Because of the time value of money (the concept that a dollar today buys more than a dollar in five years' time owing to inflation in the price of goods), an upfront discount results in a better outcome for the resident, all other things being equal. You may find some villages offer residents all the capital gain on their retirement home in return for paying a higher purchase price or ingoing contribution up front. Except in rare cases, this model favours only the village operator and unfairly pushes the risk of achieving capital growth onto the resident. Furthermore, under this model the resident is usually responsible for the entire costs of refurbishing the unit at exit.

---

### *Paying more for the capital gain*

One of my clients was thinking about buying a two-bedroom unit in a retirement village in Queensland. The unit price was $400 000, with no entitlement to any capital gain on resale or, for $480 000 (an additional 20 per cent on the purchase price), she could have a half share of the capital gain (if any). The deferred management fee was 30 per cent of the original purchase price over five years, apportioned as 7 per cent per year.

In this instance, I advised my client not to consider the option with the higher purchase price simply to get a share of the capital gains.

The additional 20 per cent on the purchase price, combined with the 30 per cent deferred fee, to acquire an entitlement

---

---

### *Paying more for the capital gain (cont'd)*

to only half of the capital gains meant the unit would have to experience capital growth of around 13 per cent *per year* simply to recoup the original outlay of $480 000 at the end of year 10. The chances of annual capital growth of 13 per cent over 10 years are remote, even in a strongly performing property market.

Furthermore, after 10 years, the original $480 000 outlay would be worth closer to $340 000 because of the value of money decreasing over time (assuming annual inflation of around 3 per cent).

Always be wary of village operators offering you the capital growth upside in return for a higher upfront price, as it will rarely make financial sense to do so.

---

## Chapter summary

- The best way to analyse a purchase price is to derive a cost per square metre for the unit and a selection of comparable properties.

- You derive a cost per square metre by dividing the asking or sale price of a property by the total square metres of its internal built area.

- The defined area typically considers internal floor space only and does not include balconies, pergolas, garages and decking.

- The square metre calculation also does not include land area, so if you are comparing detached or semi-detached retirement houses or villas, remember to include land area in your considerations, but not your calculations.

- To help you compare various purchase contracts, log in to the members' section of our website <www.findmy retirementhome.com.au> to access the online Contract Comparison Calculator.

- When negotiating your purchase contract, you are always better off negotiating an upfront discount on the purchase price rather than a lower deferred fee or a higher share of capital gain.

- The key variables to a deferred fee contract are:
  - the calculation base
  - the actual deferred fee amount
  - the years charged
  - the percentage charge incurred each year
  - the share of the capital gain.
- Other factors which can influence your financial outcome from the contract, but may not necessarily form part of the contract, include:
  - village fees
  - sales commissions or marketing costs on sale of unit
  - stamp duty
  - capital growth.
- When negotiating your contract, try to achieve a break-even point (where you recoup your ingoing contribution) as early in your tenure as possible.
- Because of the time value of money, you are always better off getting your discount upfront on the purchase price, rather than at the back end with, say, a lower exit fee.

# Chapter 13

## Capital growth

The capital growth of your retirement unit can have a huge impact on the financial outcome of your purchase when you exit the village. Good capital growth will largely offset the deferred management fee and help you to recoup as much of your original outlay as possible. Occasionally you may even make a little money from the resale of your unit!

It is important to reiterate, however, that buying a home in a retirement village is not an investment—it is a lifestyle choice. It is rare to make money from the transaction and this should never be your intention.

### What is capital growth?

Capital growth or capital gain represents the positive difference between the initial purchase price of a unit and its resale price when the resident vacates. For example, if a unit was purchased for $100 000 and resold five years later for $150 000, the capital gain would be $50 000. Capital growth in retirement communities is thought to mirror that of the surrounding residential property sector, so the price of a two-bedroom unit in a particular retirement community should be comparable to that of a two-bedroom unit of equivalent standard in the surrounding suburbs.

The factors that suppress capital growth in retirement communities are:

- The market for resales is limited to over-55s.
- There may be other limiting factors such as a no-pets policy.

- A retirement village has higher ongoing fees when compared with a residential property.

In contrast, the characteristics that support capital growth in retirement communities include:

- a limited supply in a market with strongly growing demand
- the rapid growth of the potential market for over-55s accommodation.

As with residential property, some retirement communities are going to appreciate in value faster than others because they have better features or a superior location. It is reasonable to expect that the features that accelerate growth in retirement properties are largely similar to those in the residential property sector. These can be summarised as a 'well-presented product in a popular location, with easy access to public transport and shops'.

## Factors influencing capital growth

When purchasing retirement properties, however, there are some additional features to consider if you want to increase the possibility of capital growth.

## Location

Location, location, location is important, important, important!

For your best chance at capital growth, make sure your chosen complex is well located near shops, public transport, medical centres and community facilities such as libraries and clubs. It also helps if the local area generally, and the retirement village site specifically, is flat and easily accessed by walking or motorised scooters. Complexes situated on steep slopes or gradients are avoided by over-55s, as it is difficult for them to get around if they have mobility issues.

Villages located in popular lifestyle areas such as coastal strips are also likely to be more popular and therefore generate a higher resale price. Similarly, properties with good views are highly sought after. Look for a unit with a standout feature that differentiates it from the other units in the complex, as this will help you to sell the property faster, and at a better price, when you leave. More about this later in the chapter.

## The dwelling

All other things being equal, a new house or unit with modern facilities will appreciate faster than an older-style property. Retirement living properties in Australia have typically been dominated by brick veneer and roof tile on slab construction. Instead, look for a point of difference in the construction of your preferred village, such as architectural features, superior fittings, and contemporary or architectural design.

Retirement houses or units most in demand feature single-level living, air conditioning or heating (depending on your location), emergency call facilities, wider doorways for wheelchair access and on-site management. Security should also be enhanced with dead bolts and peepholes in the doors, window locks and security screens.

## Village size

The ideal size for a retirement living community is a complex argument! Large communities typically offer more facilities such as swimming pools, bowling greens and clubhouses, which can make the complex more attractive to buyers. Weekly fees may also be lower as there are more residents to service the levies.

However, more units means more competition for buyers when it comes time to leave the community and resell the unit. As a rule of thumb, if we take the industry average length of stay in a retirement village of 10 years, we can estimate that around 10 per cent of the units in the village are resold each year—that's 10 units in a complex of 100 units, at almost one per month. If we then assume an average sales period for each unit of three months, the complex could have up to three units for sale at any time during the year. Keep in mind that more resale competition means downward pressure on resale prices.

For the purposes of this calculation I have assumed an average across the entire village, but in reality different unit types experience different levels of demand. For example, two- and three-bedroom villas are usually the most popular styles of home in a retirement village and have waiting lists of people wanting to buy them, whereas two–bedroom units are not as popular (and there are usually more of them) so there could be several vacant at any point in time.

If you do choose to live in a large complex, try to select a unit that has a point of difference to help it sell faster and for a better price when you resell. A point of difference could be a larger plot size, more bedrooms, better views, air conditioning, a hardstand area or more car spaces in the garage.

---

### Average unit resale time

When doing your due diligence on a retirement village, be sure to ask what the average resale time is for their units. Compare this with the resale times for other retirement villages nearby and you will get a good indication of which complex is more popular. Also, be aware that some types of dwellings may be in more demand than others. For example, a two-bedroom unit may not resell as quickly as a three-bedroom unit. Three months or more is the accepted industry average sale time for retirement units. Off-the-plan units in retirement villages tend to sell a lot more slowly than units in existing villages. It seems that retirees simply will not buy a property they cannot see!

---

## Sharing capital gains

Most retirement villages in Australia sell their units under a DMF contract, which typically includes an obligation for the departing resident to share any capital gains from the resale with village owner, or entirely forfeit them. The contract will state that when a resident vacates the unit and it is resold, the outgoing resident will pay to the village owner the accrued management fee, which has been deferred until exit, as well as a share (or all) of the capital gains (if any). You can read more about this fee back in chapter 11.

The owner may claim 100 per cent of the capital gain or none at all. There is no industry standard for this. However, the generally accepted industry practice seems to be an equal split (50/50) between owner and resident.

# Impact of capital growth on your DMF contract

Any capital gain realised upon resale of the unit that is retained by you is going to have a positive impact on your overall financial outcome when you leave. Therefore potential purchasers of retirement units should negotiate as high a share of the capital gain as they can.

Deferred fee and capital gain contracts vary widely between villages and even within villages, making it hard to compare apples with apples. My experience has shown that with a standard DMF contract of a 25 per cent deferred management fee over 10 years and an equal split of capital gains between the village owner and resident, a unit would need annual capital growth of around 8 per cent for a resident to break even after eight years.

Put simply, after about eight years under this style of contract, residents should be able to exit the village and recoup all of their original purchase price, weekly village fees and other costs. For an exit after year eight, the resident could well make a small profit from the transaction.

We can conclude that the capital growth of your unit over time has a major impact on your financial outcome when you leave the village. The problem with capital growth, however, is that it rarely increases in a stable way. The property market is largely cyclical: typically values rise and fall over a seven- to ten-year cycle. Timing, then, becomes important, because if you buy at the top of the cycle you may have a 10-year wait for values to grow beyond your original purchase price.

As a starting point, you can assess the reasonableness of the annual deferred fee charge in relation to the forecast capital growth for the property, in that the annual DMF percentage should not exceed the annual capital growth forecast percentage for that area. For example, if your annual deferred fee charge is 2.5 per cent and your unit experiences annual capital growth of just 3 per cent, then you will likely exit the contract having broken even.

Table 13.1 (overleaf) shows the impact of capital growth on a DMF contract.

Table 13.1: impact of capital growth on a DMF contract

| | Example 1 | Example 2 | Example 3 | Example 4 |
|---|---|---|---|---|
| Resale (exit) price | $972k | $666k | $661k | $548k |
| Years of occupation | 10 | 10 | 5 | 5 |
| Capital growth (p.a.) | 8% | 4% | 8% | 4% |
| Village return | $373k | $220k | $161k | $104k |
| Resident outcome after resale | $598k | $446k | $499k | $443k |
| | 33% | −1% | 11% | −2% |

Again, as in chapter 11, we are using the standard DMF contract of 25 over 10, or a 25 per cent deferred fee, capped at 10 years, with the fee incurred equally each year. The DMF is calculated on the purchase price (in this case assumed at $450 000), and any capital gain is split equally with the village owner.

Example 1 assumes annual capital growth of 8 per cent, for a sale price after 10 years of $972 000, which would yield the outgoing owner a 33 per cent increase on their original purchase price after the deferred fees have been removed and half the capital gain is paid to the village owner. Example 2 uses exactly the same parameters except for the capital growth assumption, which is halved to 4 per cent per year. This has reduced the resident's outcome to a loss of 1 per cent on the purchase price.

The next two examples clearly demonstrate the impact of time. Example 3 uses the original parameters with capital growth per year of 8 per cent, but we have halved the time in residence to five years. The resident here is still in front by 11 per cent after five years. In example 4, however, after only five years of occupation the capital growth has not had time to work its magic, so the resident makes a loss of around 2 per cent on the original purchase price.

You can therefore see that with an annual capital growth rate that exceeds the deferred fee incurred each year, which in this case is

2.5 per cent, you are going to lose less money than if you choose a village with poor capital growth prospects.

## Assessing potential for capital growth

I hope I have now convinced you that capital growth is important to a good financial outcome at exit, but how can you find the capital growth prospects for the particular area where you are thinking of buying a retirement home?

Forecasting capital growth for an area is a specialist art, and I call it an art because it definitely isn't a science! No one can guarantee capital growth, and there are many factors that can influence it positively or negatively.

Some organisations, however, do attempt to forecast capital growth or at least use historical rates of growth to make capital growth projections for a particular area.

### Residex

Residex <www.residex.com.au> is a well-known Australian property forecaster that produces a report called the *Postcode Explorer*, which you can access for around $90. This report, as illustrated in figure 13.1 (overleaf), will advise you of past capital growth as well as make future projections over five and eight years.

### Australian Property Monitors

Australian Property Monitors (APM) runs a website called the Home Price Guide <www.homepriceguide.com.au>, which produces a number of reports, including Postcode Reports and individual Property Reports (see figure 13.2 on p.127). Neither of these will give you a nice, convenient 10-year forecast as a Residex report will, but they do review previous years, and by taking an average of these figures, you can estimate growth going forward with reasonable confidence.

Figure 13.1: Residex *Postcode Explorer* report

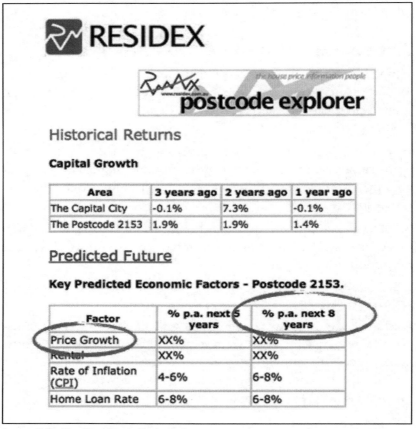

Source: © Residex. Reproduced with permission.

# RP Data

RP Data <www.myrpdata.com.au> is the market heavyweight in property reporting. While their focus is on the Professional Property Market, they produce a number of property and suburb reports. The report you want here is an Individual Property Report, as shown in figure 13.3. Like the APM report, rather than forecasting capital growth, it shows the growth achieved over prior years. You can then use this information to make your own assessment of capital growth.

Figure 13.2: APM Property Report

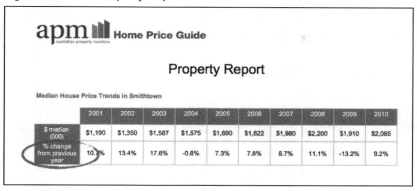

Source: Australian Property Monitors 2011.

Figure13.3: RP Data Individual Property Report

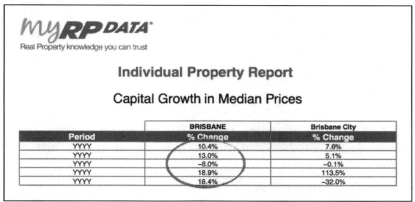

Source: © RP Data. Reproduced with permission.

Another quick and easy way to get an indication of capital growth is to buy a copy of *Australian Property Investor* or *Your Investment Property* from a newsagent. These magazines have a section at the back that details all the suburbs in the country and lists the average annual capital growth percentage for the past 10 years as well as the previous 12 months. Unfortunately the magazines do not contain capital growth forecasts, so again you need to use the previous 10 years as a guide and make your own assumptions as to whether or not this figure is reasonable.

Alternatively, you can always ask the retirement village itself about their capital growth track record. Good sales agents will monitor this information and use it as a selling point for potential residents.

## Chapter summary

- Capital growth or capital gain is the positive difference between the initial purchase price of a unit and the resale price when the resident vacates. Capital growth in retirement communities is thought to mirror that of the surrounding residential property sector, so the price of a two-bedroom unit in a particular retirement community would be similar to that of a two-bedroom unit of equivalent standard in the neighbouring suburbs.
- The features that accelerate growth in retirement properties are largely similar to those that apply in the residential property sector; they can be summarised as a 'well-presented product in a popular location, with easy access to public transport and shops'.
- When buying retirement properties, however, additional features that you should consider if you want to increase the possibility of capital growth are:
  - location
  - the dwelling
  - village size.
- You can source information about the capital growth prospects of the suburb in which your retirement village is located by buying property reports from reporters such as Residex, APM or RP Data.

# Chapter 14
## Buying off the plan

For villages that are under construction or are staging the development of additional units over time, it is standard practice to sell units off the plan, or before they have even been built. Through this strategy developers can secure pre-commitments that guarantee the viability of the project and reassure their lenders. At the same time, the purchaser can, in theory, secure a property at today's prices in a rapidly rising market, although savvy developers will seek to fix a component of estimated future capital gain into the purchase price.

Off-the-plan sales in the residential sector generally require a 10 per cent deposit, deposit bond or bank guarantee. In the retirement living sector deposit amounts are much more reasonable — sometimes just a few thousand dollars, payable once contracts are exchanged — although, unlike in the residential sector, they generally do not form a binding contract. Final payment is due on completion of the building and settlement of the contract.

Deposits on freehold retirement units are similar to standard residential properties, at around 5 to 10 per cent of the overall purchase price. One trap on freehold properties bought off the plan is that stamp duty on the full purchase amount has to be paid shortly after the exchange of contracts, which can occur well before settlement of the property. For the high-end, luxury properties this could mean a payment of $20 000–$30 000, which most retirees do not have readily available in their bank accounts.

## Advantages of buying off the plan

For purchasers there can be advantages to buying off the plan:

- It locks in the price for the new home.
- The buyer may be able to exercise more control over finishes, floor plans and interior style, and vary aspects of the finished product, such as upgrading benchtops, carpets or tiling, and whitegoods.
- The buyer gets a wider choice of units or villas, whereas an existing community can offer only whatever is vacant at the time.
- There is more time for retirees to sell their existing home before moving into the retirement village.
- The developer may be under pressure to sell stock to satisfy bank covenants or fund the next stage of development, meaning you can negotiate a better price.
- The developer could be keen to do a deal.
- Developers are not emotionally attached to the units and are more comfortable selling than someone who has actually lived in the property.
- Developers generally have a reasonable price expectation, whereas owner–occupiers may not.
- The buyer gets a builder's guarantee, which last up to seven years.
- New homes have lower maintenance costs.

## Disadvantages of buying off the plan

There are some disadvantages for the purchaser, however:

- The buyer is vulnerable to fluctuations in price, which is good if prices increase, but bad if they decrease.
- The purchaser buys the property sight unseen.
- Construction or weather problems may delay delivery.
- The purchaser has little control over the final quality and look of the outside of the complex.
- Purchasers may not be allowed to inspect the construction work in progress.

- Contracts rarely include penalties for late completion by the developer.

- There are no retained portions of the purchase price to ensure rectification of any defects.

There are many risks in acquiring a property that cannot be inspected. For example, the purchaser cannot be sure of what the property will look like, the standard of finishes, the practical layout, the size and dimensions (including ceiling height), or the view or outlook. These drawbacks can be partially overcome by viewing an existing or demonstration unit, video presentations or sample finishes. However, the buyer should attempt to anticipate any ancillary issues that could arise with a new development. Apart from the unit itself, consider issues such as the style, appearance and finish of common areas, the likely noise from other units or roads, the proposed security system, visitor parking, access to garages, ventilation, garbage disposal and landscaping.

In addition to the aesthetic issues there may be financial factors that the purchaser will find difficult to anticipate. These include the actual market value of the property when completed and estimates of the maintenance contributions that will be payable.

## Off-the-plan contracts

Purchasing off the plan can be more complex than acquiring an existing property. As a rule, your contract should include:

- a specific obligation on the vendor to construct the building

- a copy of the draft strata plan showing the lot and any garage, car space, storeroom and so on.

- a scale plan of the interior of the unit showing internal improvements

- a copy of the approved plans and specifications

- a schedule of the finishes and appliances

- a description of the title proposed to be registered

- the obligation of the vendor to construct using new materials, in a proper and workmanlike manner and within a specified time frame

- a mechanism in the contract to deal with variations
- a dispute resolution procedure
- a rectification provision (typically this will provide for the vendor to rectify defects that arise within, say, three months but will exclude shrinkage or minor settlement cracks).

Most of these inclusions are applicable to off-the-plan freehold and leasehold properties but not to retirement village contracts for dwellings you do not own.

## Accepting handover of your new unit

Before settling on your contract and accepting handover of your new unit from the developer, you need to make sure you are getting everything you are entitled to under your contract.

### Home inspection services

A useful service to assist with this is offered by Archicentre, the building advisory service of the Royal Australian Institute of Architects, who can provide advice on building plans. Archicentre can prepare a report that includes an opinion on whether the rooms are of a reasonable size, the quality of the fixture and fittings, and the layout.

When construction is complete, but before you hand over any money to settle the property, Archicentre can conduct a practical completion inspection on your behalf, including checking the building specifications against the plans, confirming that the promised fixtures and fittings have been included, and commenting on the overall standard of the building. Each of these services costs around $400, depending on the location and extent of work involved.

Handovers.com also provides a service to inspect and accept practical completion of your retirement home, and its services is cheaper than Archicentre's.

You can find the contact details for Archicentre and Handovers. com in the links and resources contained in chapter 20.

Precautions you should take when buying off the plan include:

- Only buy from developers with a good reputation. Ask to see other sites previously completed by the developer and inspect the quality of work as well as speaking with existing village residents. Avoid local developers who have decided to have a crack at retirement villages, because their residential sales are slow!

- Avoid off-the-plan projects unless construction has begun. There is too much risk in paying a deposit to a developer for a site that may not even be built on, for whatever reason.

- Try to include a clause in which the developer pays you a penalty if the property is not completed by an agreed time (known as liquidated damages).

- Specify every detail in the contract, including fixtures and fittings. For example, do not accept a 'stainless steel oven'; specify a particular brand and model of stainless steel oven.

- Make sure the unit will be ready for your occupation by the time you sell and move out of your house.

Early entrants into a village with future staged development have to put up with construction noise, dust and inconvenience every time a new stage is begun. However, if you can deal with this, there are good discounts to be negotiated with developers who are keen to sell homes to fund the next stage of works. A typical strategy for developers is to start selling units at a low price and to increase the prices over time as sales progress. This serves to get initial sales away, but also creates the impression of capital growth for future buyers.

There may be no guarantee that additional stages are built within a particular time frame, or built at all. So you should be careful not to base your decision on village facilities that may be constructed at a later date, unless there are ironclad guarantees from the developer in the contract that they will be completed by a certain date.

Use the following checklist before making a decision to pay any money or sign any contract for retirement village accommodation that has not yet been constructed or is not yet ready for occupation:

- Make sure you do not sell your current home too early, leaving you without accommodation.

- Discuss your purchase with people you trust.

- Understand the type of contractual arrangement under which you will be entering the village (i.e. loan/licence, leasehold, rental, company title or a freehold strata scheme).

- Make sure a suitably experienced solicitor closely examines any contract offered in connection with the sale of the unit.

- Make sure the contract gives you proper protection in the event of something going wrong either with the completion of the village or with your own circumstances.

- Do not pay too much money up front as a deposit, and check the likely standard by looking at other villages built by the operator or builder concerned.

- Check whether you can make customised changes (for example, the colour and style of tiles, carpets and internal painting, and the types of stoves and dishwashers).

- Check whether you can visit the village during construction.

- Confirm that you have finance in place if the village is finished earlier than expected.

In part V, I will look at some of the issues surrounding the purchase of your retirement home, starting with the sale of your existing home.

## Chapter summary

- For retirement villages still under construction it is typical for residents to buy their unit off the plan.

- Buying off the plan is more complex than buying an existing retirement village unit.

- There are both advantages and disadvantages to buying off the plan. If you are thinking about buying a unit off the plan, you should consider the advantages and disadvantages carefully according to your own personal circumstances.

- Get expert advice from either Archicentre or Handovers.com before accepting handover of your new, off-the-plan retirement unit.

# PART V

# The purchase

In this part I will cover the issues specific to the purchase of a retirement home.

I start by looking at the sale of your existing home, as in most cases the proceeds from this transaction are used to fund the purchase of the new retirement home. I will then look at some of the issues that are unique to retirement home contracts. Finally I will get into the nuts and bolts of negotiating your contract, including the key contract terms you need to look out for—and to change if they are not acceptable to you. The information in this part will save you a lot of heartache during and after your stay in the village!

# Chapter 15
## Selling your home

Research shows that when people buy a retirement home they need to sell their principal place of residence to fund their purchase. Typically this is the family home where they have lived for many years and raised their children. The sale of the family home is an important step towards unlocking cash for the purchase of a retirement home, as well as funding retirement income or lifestyle purchases.

Deciding to sell the family home, with all the memories attached to it, can be a very emotional experience. If you have lived in the same place for many years it is likely you will have a network of local friends, medical support and preferred shopping haunts. However, it is usually the right decision. Among the most persuasive reasons for this are:

- The house is too large for your current needs.
- The house needs considerable ongoing maintenance.
- The house has accessibility problems, with different levels and stairs.
- The yard and gardens require too much work.
- You need to sell the property to release some cash for living, lifestyle or travel.

### Making the decision to sell

It is important not to leave the decision to move into a retirement home too late. Moving is stressful and it gets harder to deal with this stress as you get older. Often people put off the decision to move until it is virtually forced on them by circumstance, such as a bad fall or the need to unlock cash to support your retirement. So make your decision early and involve everyone whose advice you value and trust.

## The market is flat—should I sell?

If you are putting off moving to a retirement community because you are waiting for your house to go up in value (and therefore make you more money on the sale), then you may be operating under a flawed assumption!

It is common for people to say that the market is flat or weak, and that they are not going to sell because they won't get the price they think their property is worth. This means waiting until the market improves and prices increase, which can take years.

This is a mistaken although commonly held view. People see the inflated prices that similar properties sold for during the heat of the last property boom and think their house should be worth the same price. However, this is rarely the case. It is hard to time your transactions perfectly so that you sell at the market peak and buy in the trough. Property indicators such as median house prices, new home approvals or new finance approvals look back at past events, not at future events. By the time you have figured out that the market has peaked or bottomed, the data is already several months old and you have missed your opportunity.

The approach taken by sophisticated property investors is that even though you may be selling into a softer market, you are concurrently buying into that same soft market. This means that while you may not get a boom-time price for your property, you will likely pay a lower price for the property you end up buying because it is in the same stage of the market as your home.

In other words, if you sell into a hot market you will buy into a hot market; and if you sell into a flat market you will buy into a flat market. All other things being equal, the money you leave on the table from the sale of your home you should make back when you purchase your new home. This is actually more efficient financially anyway, because on the sell side, your agent's fees are lower, as is your capital gains tax (if it is an investment property you are selling).

On the buy side, you pay less stamp duty on a cheaper buy price (assuming your new purchase is freehold and not a leasehold or DMF property).

# Selling your home—DIY or use an agent?

The ideal outcome for you as a vendor is to sell your home for the highest possible price in the shortest possible time. The best way to achieve this outcome is to expose your property to the maximum number of potential buyers at the same time. For this you can either use an agent or do it yourself. Selling your home is not rocket science and with the assistance of a good property solicitor you should be able to do it yourself. It will take a commitment of time, however, and you should be confident in your negotiating and marketing skills.

The pros and cons of each approach are summarised in tables 15.1 and 15.2 (overleaf).

Table 15.1: advantages and disadvantages of using an agent to sell your house

| Advantages | Disadvantages |
|---|---|
| Agents are experts in selling homes. | Agent commissions are payable so it's more expensive. |
| Agents look after all the details. | You still need to find a good agent. |
| A significantly lower time commitment is required from the seller. | Agents' interests may not be aligned with yours. |
| The agent answers and screens buyer calls. | Any marketing promotes the agent as well as the property. |
| Advertising and marketing is of better quality. | You don't know what the agent is saying about your property. |
| Buyer inspections are screened and supervised. | Incompetent agents may damage your sale prospects. |

Table 15.2: advantages and disadvantages of selling your house yourself

| Advantages | Disadvantages |
|---|---|
| No commissions means it's cheaper. | It needs a big time commitment. |
| You have control of the process. | You lack the experience of an agent. |
| You negotiate the price you will accept directly with a buyer. | You must negotiate the price you will accept. |
| You won't get bullied into accepting a low price. | You must answer and screen all buyer calls. |
| You control what information prospective buyers see and hear. | Advertising and marketing will probably be more expensive (no bulk buyer leverage). |
| You can proceed at your own pace. | You must supervise buyer inspections (time and security). |

Unless you have the time and confidence to sell your home personally, my advice is to use a real estate agent but to make sure you understand the process, including their legal obligations to you and how best to work with your agent to achieve an optimal outcome. Real estate agents are experts in the marketing of property and negotiating sales and are, in my view, a necessary part of the sales process.

If you choose to do it yourself, however, there are now plenty of resources available on the internet to assist you.

## Real estate agents

The Real Estate Institute of Australia summarises the basic job of a real estate agent as 'to sell your home for the best price possible, as quickly as possible'. To do this, agents deliver a range of services from the early stages to the final settlement, including:

- advice on the sale price you can expect for your property
- advice on whether you should sell by private treaty or at auction

- advertising and marketing of your property
- bringing your home before potential purchasers
- negotiating the selling price between you and the purchaser
- facilitating the actual sale of your property and the final exchange of contracts.

In return for these services, agents seek a fee for the time and costs involved in selling your property.

The key to all of this, however, is finding a good agent!

## More advantages to using an agent

More advantages to using an agent include:

- *Security*. It is unwise to invite a stranger into your home. An agent can do the screening of potential customers and accompany them on the inspection.

- *Consumer protection*. The consumer has the full protection of state legislation governing real estate transactions.

- *Time*. Agents are trained to qualify customers and handle them quickly and efficiently, thereby finalising a faster transaction.

- *Reduces conflict*. The primary role of the agent is to act as a third party go-between for the seller and the purchaser. This function can reduce personality conflicts, cultural differences and clashes of ego that may occur between the seller and purchaser.

- *Negotiation skills*. Agents are trained negotiators who will seek a mutually agreeable outcome for the seller and purchaser.

- *Advertising more cost effective*. Agencies negotiate bulk media packages across a variety of different media, so they can leverage substantial discounts for you as the seller.

- *Access to major internet sites*. Most prospective purchasers use the internet to search for a property. Agents know the best websites to use and have access to them at far cheaper rates than a private individual.

> ### *More advantages to using an agent (cont'd)*
>
> - *No results, no commission.* Agents get paid only for results. There are very few professions that can offer a range of services similar to that of an agent without charging a fee for their time.
>
> - *Market price.* The agent has a duty at law to achieve the best price for the seller. They also have a duty to fully investigate the market on behalf of the seller and to keep the seller informed about market trends. Customers are less likely to make unrealistic offers to an agent.

In the members' section of our website (accessed by clicking the 'Members' link and using the password noted in the introduction) I have posted a bonus chapter, 'How to sell your home', designed to help you through the process of selling your home. Topics covered include:

- selecting an agent
- appointing an agent
- types of appointments
- commissions and fees
- methods of sale
- marketing
- presenting your home.

## Chapter summary

- The sale of the family home is an important step towards unlocking cash for the purchase of a retirement home, as well as funding retirement.

- It is important not to leave the decision to move into a retirement home too late. Moving is stressful and it gets harder to deal with stress as you get older.

- It is common for people to put off selling the family home when the market is flat and they believe they won't get the right price for their property.

- The approach taken by sophisticated property investors is that even though you may be selling into a softer market, you are concurrently buying into that same soft market.

- It is not difficult to sell your own home rather than using a real estate agent; however, I recommend you use an agent, as they are experts in selling houses.

- Our free membership website has a bonus chapter for readers about selling your home.

# Chapter 16

## Contract time!

In this chapter I will look at some of the important issues around receiving and executing your purchase contract. As already noted in chapter 2, the ability of the village operator to structure its relationship with you as resident is greatest at the time of contracting, so this is the time for you to get it right. It is no use signing the contract and then trying to negotiate your concerns with the operator, as there is no incentive for them to change any of the clauses. Similarly, you cannot plead ignorance when you decide to leave the village and only then realise the impact of the fees and charges. You must agree to all changes with the village operator before you sign the purchase contract.

## Waiting lists

Before reaching contract stage, if your preferred retirement village is full you may have to go onto a waiting list until space becomes available. Waiting lists are used in popular villages with strong demand from potential residents.

Ideally the practice of using waiting lists allows for an open and transparent method of treating potential residents fairly and honestly. If you are asked to sign onto a waiting list, you are within your rights to request a copy of the village waiting list policy, although there is no guarantee there will be one.

Some villages charge a fee for being placed on their waiting list, as this helps to qualify potential buyers and identify individuals who are serious about moving into the village. This is an acceptable market practice and the fee is usually only a couple of hundred dollars.

Waiting list protocols are not always covered in state retirement villages legislation, so you should be careful to ensure that:

- you are given a receipt if there is a charge for being placed on the waiting list
- the waiting list fee is fully refundable if you choose to withdraw from the list
- the waiting list protocol is fair and honest.

Once you have found a unit and agreed on a price with the village sales agent, you may be asked to meet with the village manager for an interview.

## Interview

If you thought your days of sitting through interviews were over, then you were mistaken! Most retirement villages require potential residents to be interviewed by the village manager to ensure they are suitable candidates for the complex. Although this interview may be largely a formality, the manager does have the power to refuse entry to those judged not to be a suitable fit.

Interviewing potential residents is actually a good practice, as it serves to weed out any applicants who might cause problems for existing residents.

Once you have passed your interview with the village manager, you may be asked for a deposit.

## Deposits

As noted in chapter 11, some retirement communities take deposits of a thousand dollars or more to register your interest in a particular property. The deposit may or may not actually hold the unit for you. Some villages will take multiple deposits on one property and give the property to the first buyer who can settle the contract with the vendor. As most purchase contracts are conditional on the sale of your home, this usually means that whoever can sell their house first can settle first!

Always ask to view the village deposit policy, and never put a deposit on a property unless you have a written guarantee that it is fully refundable in the event that either you or the village owner decides to withdraw from the sale. You will avoid later disappointment if you clearly understand at the outset whether or not the deposit actually holds the unit.

The next stage of the process is to sign a purchase contract.

## Contracts

Purchase contracts are different for each type of purchase arrangement. Back in chapter 9, I identified the three main retirement village purchase arrangements as freehold, leasehold and deferred management fee (loan/lease or loan/licence). The main inclusions in the contract package for each of these purchase arrangements are as follows:

- *Freehold*. Freehold contracts include a purchase contract and the by-laws associated with the community titles scheme that governs the operation of the village. If the village offers freehold title but is also a registered retirement village (you will know this because they are applying deferred management fees to the purchase arrangement), then the contract package should include a disclosure statement, as required under state retirement villages legislation.

- *Leasehold*. Leasehold contracts include the purchase agreement for the house or built structure that exists on the land, along with a lease agreement for the plot of land on which the house sits. In addition, the contract should include a copy of the strata community by-laws or rules that apply to the village.

- *Deferred management fee (loan/lease or loan/licence)*. DMF contracts include a purchase agreement in the form of a lease or licence agreement, a disclosure statement (as required under the state retirement villages legislation) and the village rules.

All these inclusions make for a very thick and seemingly complex contract package! Table 16.1 (overleaf) summarises the inclusions for each type of contract.

Table 16.1 retirement home contract packages

| Purchase arrangement | Contract inclusions |
|---|---|
| Freehold | Purchase contract |
| | Disclosure statement (if it is a registered retirement village) |
| | Body corporate (Queensland) or owners corporation by-laws |
| Leasehold | Purchase contract for the built structure |
| | Lease for the land area |
| | Body corporate (Queensland) or owners corporation by-laws |
| DMF (loan/lease or loan/licence) | Purchase contract (lease or licence) |
| | Disclosure statement |
| | Village rules |

# Disclosure statements

Registered retirement villages have an obligation under the retirement villages legislation to supply purchasers with a document known as a disclosure statement or public information document (PID), depending on the state you live in. This document contains vital information about the village that the owner–operator is obliged by law to disclose to a prospective buyer. It is usually required to be attached to the purchase contract and takes precedence over any discrepancies that may exist between it and the purchase agreement, although understandably any anomalies between the disclosure statement and the retirement villages legislation are overridden by the legislation.

Disclosure documents should contain information such as:

- size and location of the village
- services and facilities
- proximity to hospitals, shops, public transport and other services

- type of purchase contract (for example, loan/lease or loan/licence)
- identity and contact details of the owner–operator
- security measures
- financial details
- residents' committee details.

Other information worth asking for and investigating includes:

- *Village site plan.* The village site plan will show the location of the services and facilities of the village in relation to the unit you are looking to buy. The site plan should also indicate any future development plans so you can consider your exposure to the noise and dust associated with construction.

- *Village rules.* All retirement villages have their own set of rules or by-laws that residents must comply with. Check them out early to make sure there is nothing there that would give you concern. For example, if you like tinkering with your car engine you may find the village rules do not allow you to perform this kind of work on site.

- *Minutes from recent residents' committee meetings.* Check the minutes to get a feel for the kind of issues discussed. The minutes will also give you an indication of whether the residents' committee is effective or dysfunctional.

- *Copies of the contract to be used for the purchase.* Always obtain a copy of the contract and go through it in detail before signing anything. Should you decide to proceed with the purchase, I recommend you get a solicitor who is experienced with retirement village contracts to review your contract as well.

- *Floor plans and price list of the available residences.* Comparing floor plans and prices will allow you to see the value of that additional room or living space.

- *Village operating budget.* Reviewing a copy of the village operating budget for the past few years will give you a feel for the annual cost increases that have been applied to your village fee, as well as an indication of the fiscal discipline of the village operator and residents' committee.

- *Village development plan.* Check whether there are any further stages due to be developed. Construction noise can interfere with a peaceful retirement and additional units can also affect the resale price of your unit, if you are competing with newer homes.

- *Waiting list policy.* If you are putting your name down on a waiting list you need to find out how the list operates. Does it guarantee you a unit? Will they cross you off the list if you take too long to make up your mind?

- *Village capital replacement plan and maintenance fund.* The sinking fund for the village is responsible for the maintenance and refurbishment of the common areas and is funded by levies on all residents. How have these levies been derived? Is there an engineering or quantity surveyor's report to back up the cost estimates?

- *Community scheme by-laws and minutes.* If the village is a strata-titled freehold scheme, ask for a copy of scheme by-laws and the minutes from the last general meeting.

- *Company constitution.* If the village is a company-titled scheme, ask for a copy of the company constitution.

## Contract process

The village sales agent will be able to explain the contract process that applies to the village you have selected. Table 16.2 shows a typical time line.

Table 16.2: contract process

| Order | Event |
| --- | --- |
| 1 | Purchaser signs an expression of interest |
| 2 | Purchaser receives and reviews contract documents |
| 3 | Purchaser signs contracts and pays deposit |
| 4 | Seller signs contracts |
| 5 | Cooling-off period starts |

| 6 | Cooling-off period ends |
|---|---|
| 7 | Contract conditions are met |
| 8 | Contract settles—final payment made |
| 9 | Resident moves in |

You should always use a solicitor for the conveyancing of your retirement home purchase contract. Choose your legal counsel wisely, because most solicitors have probably never seen one of these contracts before and they need to be familiar with the state retirement villages legislation for the region in which you want to buy. In the members' section of our website, accessed using the login details outlined in the introduction, I have provided a list of solicitors in each state who I know are experienced with retirement village contracts. (In case you were wondering, I don't get any commissions for these referrals!) Some of these solicitors also represent retirement village operators. Be sure to check if your solicitor represents the operator of your particular village; if so, use someone else.

## Cooling-off or settling-in period

For registered retirement villages, most state retirement villages legislation now includes a provision for a period of cooling off during which buyers can successfully terminate their contract.

The cooling-off or settling-in period is specified in the legislation and typically commences from the signing of the contract by either the buyer or the seller, or the date on which a resident occupies the unit (depending on the state). During this period the resident is free to terminate the contract. Termination may incur some minor penalties or payments, such as an agreed rental amount for the period of the cooling-off time that the unit was off the market. Make a diary note for a week or two before the end of the cooling-off period to review whether or not you want to exercise this right.

Table 16.3 (overleaf) shows some state-specific cooling-off periods, although as you would expect there are particular conditions attached to each one.

Table 16.3: cooling-off periods

| State | Days |
|---|:---:|
| Queensland | 14 |
| New South Wales | 90 |
| Victoria | 3 |
| Australian Capital Territory | 5 |
| Tasmania | 5 |
| South Australia | 15 |
| Western Australia | 5 |

## Chapter summary

- Waiting lists are used in popular villages where there is strong demand from potential buyers.

- Retirement communities take deposits of a thousand dollars or more to register your interest in a particular property. The deposit may or may not hold the unit for you; you need to confirm this with the sales agent before handing over any money.

- Retirement villages legislation includes a provision for a cooling-off period, during which prospective buyers can successfully terminate their contract to buy a retirement unit. The cooling-off or settling-in period is usually specified in a purchase contract as commencing from the granting or execution of the occupancy right or the date a resident occupies a unit.

- You should always use a solicitor for the conveyancing of your retirement home purchase contract, as for any residential purchase. Make sure your solicitor is experienced with retirement home purchase contracts.

# Chapter 17

## Negotiating tips and key contract terms

It is worth repeating the point that the ability of a village operator to control its relationship with you as the resident is greatest at the time of drafting the purchase or occupation contract. Consequently this is the best time for you to make sure you get a fair deal—it is too late once you have moved into the village. Have your contract reviewed by a solicitor who is experienced in dealing with retirement home purchase contracts.

In this chapter I will list the key terms in your contract that you should negotiate and also explain how to set up your negotiations for the best chance of success.

### Negotiating your contract

From a negotiating point of view, positioning is everything. When you start negotiating on your retirement village unit you should aim to be in a position that gives you the best chance of success. In other words, you should have your affairs arranged in a way that gives you an advantage over the vendor, which could be the retirement village owner (or the sales agent) and/or the outgoing resident.

The strongest possible position for a buyer is to be able to deliver the fastest and cleanest purchase contract to the vendor. It is not always about price; in fact, it is often not about price.

A fast and clean contract specifically means:

• a short contract settlement period

- few, if any, conditions that must be met before settlement of the contract, such as the sale of your current home
- few, if any, changes to the contract, particularly ones that will require rewording or review by the vendor's solicitors.

To be able to deliver this kind of contract, you as the buyer should have the following:

- *Your existing house sold or under an unconditional contract.* In chapter 18 I will explain about timing your move and the stress of not having a home base between the sale of your existing home and the settlement of a new retirement home. Unfortunately, the best position to be in for your new retirement home negotiation is to have already sold your home so you can settle the new purchase quickly. This strategy is not for the fainthearted, however! If you are concerned about this risk, you can always ask for an extended period of settlement on the sale of your home, such as 60 or 90 days, to give you more time to find your new retirement home. But you should still be careful to ensure the contract of sale on your home goes unconditional as soon as possible to prevent the sale from falling over. Settlement can be brought forward much more easily (and without penalty) than it can be pushed out, in the event that you find your retirement home faster than expected.

- *More than one preferred option.* Try to find two or more properties in separate villages that you could quite happily buy. Although you will probably have only one preferred retirement home in mind, it is ideal to have more than one option for negotiating purposes. This allows you to play off one village against another and drive a better deal. Retirement village sales agents are so used to people coming into their village and simply buying with emotion that they are often unprepared and ill equipped to deal with a buyer who can negotiate.

- *Ability to settle within 30 days.* Typically it takes a considerable length of time for retirement village operators to sell a unit. Three months is around the industry average, although six to twelve months is not uncommon. It is worth noting that retirement village sales agents, like any real estate agents, may be paid a commission or bonus for the units they sell, so they are motivated to do the deal. Also remember that unless the village is brand new or being sold off the plan, the village sales agent is selling the property on behalf of the previous resident or the previous resident's estate. So if you can deliver a fast settlement on the purchase, sales agents will be keen to negotiate and to finalise the sale in order to get their commission. In this event you will get clear preference over any other purchasers who need to sell their existing home as a precondition to settling the contract.

- *Confirmed minimum acceptable purchase arrangement for each of your selected properties.* This means a clearly defined and understood position on the pricing arrangement that you are prepared to accept or walk away from. To get to this position you need to understand the contract purchase arrangements and costs intimately. Other key terms will be non-financial and will be outlined later in this chapter. In chapter 12 I explained how you can analyse the financial terms of your contract by using the Contract Comparison Calculator provided in the members' section of our website. The calculator is a quick and easy way for you to play with the various purchase terms you think you may be able to negotiate, such as purchase price or deferred fee, and immediately see what the impact of your negotiations will be on your overall financial outcome at exit.

## Understanding your negotiating position

Key to any kind of negotiation is to understand your base position and your preferred position. Here's how it works.

For a specific retirement village unit, find the purchase terms that work best for you, such as a lower fee or a discount on the purchase price. I will call this position A. Then work out the base or minimum purchase terms you would accept on this unit, which I call position B. The negotiating plan or strategy is to aim for position A, knowing that you are prepared to accept position B. Anywhere in between is a good result.

Let's look at an example of this.

## *Example: negotiating for success*

You are interested in a two-bedroom unit in the Garden of Eden Village at East Beach. The current terms on offer are a unit sale price of $395 000, with a 35 per cent deferred management fee spread over seven years and calculated on the unit's resale price on exit. There is a 50/50 split of capital gains between the outgoing resident and the village owner. The resident is also responsible for any refurbishment costs to bring the unit up to a marketable condition.

The negotiating positions are outlined in table 17.1.

Table 17.1: outline of negotiating position

| Terms | Existing | Position A (preferred) | Position B (acceptable) |
|---|---|---|---|
| Purchase price | $395 000 | $365 000 | $380 000 |
| Deferred fee | 35% over 7 years | 25% over 10 years | 35% over 10 years |
| DMF calculation | Exit | Entry | Entry |
| Share of capital gains | 50/50 | 50/50 | 50/50 |
| Refurbishment | 100% | 50/50 By negotiation | 50/50 By negotiation |

Position A in this scenario represents your preferred position: a discount of $30 000 off the purchase price and a lower deferred fee of 25 per cent calculated over 10 years on the entry price. You are comfortable with the equal sharing of capital gains, but want the refurbishment costs to be split 50/50 and the refurbishment clause to be tightened up to give you a stronger position to negotiate the scope.

Now clearly it would be foolish to expect the vendor to move on all of these points (although you never know, and you should always ask!), so you also have position B, which sets out the minimum terms you are prepared to accept, without which you would walk away from the sale. The minimum acceptable terms include a $15000 discount off the purchase price. You are okay with the 35 per cent deferred fee but will not budge on a 10-year fee spread and the calculation on the entry price as opposed to the resale price. The 50/50 share of capital gains is also acceptable but you definitely want some certainty around the refurbishment clause in the contract. With a 50/50 sharing of the capital gains you should also be seeking a 50/50 sharing of the refurbishment costs.

The effectiveness of these tactics is limited if the village has a waiting list of people ready to move in. If you try to push these villages for a better deal they may simply tell you to get lost and proceed to the next person in line! However, it is always worth a try and you may find that your ability to settle quickly is more highly valued than a higher sale price.

It is also best to avoid getting lawyers involved in the early stages of the contract negotiation. Yes, you will need a solicitor to do the contract conveyancing, as you would for any other property purchase; however, involving lawyers inevitably creates complexity and expense, and increases the time it will take to close a contract. Where possible, negotiate terms directly with the vendor and deliver an agreed position to your solicitor. For changes to contract clauses, tell your solicitor the outcome you are trying to achieve and let the expert craft the change to the clause that you then propose to the seller. Alternatively the village operator's solicitor may draft the clause changes.

The example previously outlined was based on a DMF contract negotiation, although these strategies are also effective for freehold and leasehold purchases. Again, find your preferred position and your walk-away position; aim for your preferred position, but anything inbetween your preferred position and your base position is a good outcome.

---

**Negotiating tip**

The quickest way to find out whether or not the village is likely to be negotiable on terms is to ask how long the unit has been on the market. If it has been for sale for more than three months, then you can assume that sales are soft and the vendor is negotiable—less than three months and it is less likely they will do a deal.

Skilled sales agents should never reveal how long a property has been for sale, but I have never had trouble finding out this information!

---

# Key terms for negotiation

In this section I will review the key clauses you should identify in your contract and seek to change if the terms are unacceptable to you, and consider what is and is not reasonable. Most of these terms relate to DMF contracts, but some are also relevant to freehold and leasehold purchase contracts.

## Deposit

Payment of the deposit is typically the first time money changes hands. Try to get this amount as low as possible—around $1000–$3000 is reasonable. It should be fully refundable if either party chooses not to proceed. To avoid disappointment, find out if the deposit actually holds the unit for you or simply acts as an expression of interest.

## Purchase price

Obviously the lower the purchase price or ingoing contribution the better! Because of the time value of money, it always makes sense to get a discount on your upfront purchase price rather than, for example, a reduction on the exit fee. You may be able to raise or drop your purchase price by offering to increase or decrease your DMF or share of capital gains. Some villages may offer a cash rebate on settlement rather than decreasing the purchase price, as a lower purchase price impacts on the valuation of the entire village! Negotiating a good discount on the purchase price by accepting a higher exit fee is almost always going to lead to a better financial outcome for you at exit.

## Inclusions

Instead of (or in addition to) a discount on the purchase price, for new properties you can negotiate for the developer to throw in significant inclusions such as ducted air conditioning, better quality tiles, better whitegoods, nicer floor coverings and ceiling fans. Developers prefer to do this than to drop the purchase price, as the valuation over the entire village falls if a sale on one unit is made at a lower price. This strategy applies to all new properties whether they are freehold, leasehold or DMF.

## Deferred fee percentage

The deferred management fee charged can be changed. Preferably you would want the total amount charged reduced — for example, for a 25 per cent over 10 years contract ask for 20 per cent over 10 years. A lower fee over a longer period of time is a good outcome — for example, 25 per cent or 20 per cent over 15 years — as you incur the fee in smaller annual increments and will not be penalised for an early departure.

What is a reasonable DMF? I use 25 per cent as the benchmark standard and believe this amount delivers a fair return to the village owner. If the fee were higher than this, you would want to see a reduced village fee (less than $100 per week) or some pretty amazing facilities in the complex — for example, a village bus and a nicely appointed clubhouse. The ASX-listed FKP Group is one of the largest owners and operators of retirement villages in the country. The average DMF across their portfolio is around 30 per cent, so it would appear more likely that you will find a DMF of 30 per cent to be the standard charge in retirement villages.

The DMF can be charged on the entry price (ingoing contribution) or the exit or resale price. The benefit of a fee based on the entry price is that you know exactly what your deferred fee is going to be when you leave. Typically, if the fee is charged on the exit price there should be no capital gains payable to the village owner, although in some cases they do try to get away with a share of the gain under this arrangement as well.

## Share of capital gain on resale

You should negotiate as high a share of the capital gain as possible, preferably with little or no share going to the village owner. Contracts with no share of the gain going to the village owner typically calculate the DMF on the exit or resale price, which gives the village owner their exposure to the capital gain. Contracts that charge the DMF on the resale price with no sharing of capital gains will usually deliver the best financial outcome for you at exit.

Do not accept a contract in which the deferred fee is calculated on the exit price and the village owner also takes a share of the capital gain, as this is well outside current market practice.

In chapter 11 I mentioned that some purchase contracts place an obligation on you as the outgoing resident to refund the village owner for any capital losses if the unit is sold for less than your original purchase price. This means that if, for example, you acquired your unit for $100 000 and resold it at a later date for $80 000, then you would be obliged to pay the village owner $20 000 to make up the difference. So your exit entitlement would be $80 000 less your deferred fee, your share of the refurbishment costs and any selling costs, as well as $20 000 for the resale difference!

This clause is designed to protect the village operator from residents selling their unit for an absurdly low price, perhaps in the event that they want to pass it on cheaply to a friend or relative, or perhaps to rob the village owner of a share of any capital gains. In my opinion, however, it also prevents the departing resident or the resident's estate from dropping the price of the unit in the event that the property market has softened and they need a fast sale.

I recommend that your solicitor change this clause to read that the departing resident is obliged to pay any capital loss to the village operator that is greater than 10 per cent of the original ingoing contribution. With this change, departing residents or their estate are able to meet the market and drop the price of the unit by up to 10 per cent of the original purchase price without penalty, which I believe is fair.

# Refurbishment costs and level of refurbishment

The scope of any refurbishment should not be completely at the village owner's discretion. Furthermore, contracts that give 100 per cent of the capital gain on resale of the unit to the village owner should not place any refurbishment cost obligations on the departing resident. Refurbishment costs should be split between the village owner and the resident in the same proportion as the sharing of any capital gain on resale of the unit.

As the unit owner, you should have final approval of the refurbishment scope and budget. At the very least, the scope and budget should be agreed by negotiation with the village owner and noted as such in the contract.

Remember that this kind of issue must be resolved before you sign the contract and move into the village — it is too late to try to negotiate this when you are looking to leave the village.

Some state legislation now includes a specific time frame for the village operator to complete any refurbishment work. This is a great idea as it places the burden to quickly refurbish your unit and get it back on the market squarely on the village operator. If your state does not include this provision, then you should add it to your purchase contract terms. A period of 90 days to refurbish should be a fair and acceptable condition for both parties.

# Sales commissions and marketing costs

Avoid contract clauses that lock you into using the village sales staff to sell your unit on exit, otherwise known as a controlling right to sell. It is better to keep your selling options open on this point, even though you will usually get a better outcome by using the village sales staff as they are most familiar with the contracts and are on site for walk-in enquiries. The purchase contract may stipulate the sales commission charged by the sales staff on resale of the unit. A commission of 2 to 3 per cent of the sale price is standard; however, consider leaving commissions blank at this stage so you can use a more incentivised commission structure when the time comes to sell.

Instead of a percentage sales commission, some village purchase contracts charge the outgoing resident for any marketing costs associated with selling the unit. For this clause, you need to make sure the level of refundable costs is capped and not left open for the operator to charge you whatever they want. From a negotiating point of view, put the onus on the operator to come up with a figure and negotiate it down from there. A capped amount of around 1 to 2 per cent of the sale price of your unit is fair, providing the operator is not also taking a sales commission.

Your overall selling costs, including any commissions and marketing costs, should not exceed 2 to 3 per cent of the sale price of your unit.

## Sale price

The resale price of a unit will generally be set by the village operator in conjunction with the outgoing resident or the resident's estate. If you and the village owner are unable to agree on a sale price, an independent valuer should be appointed to determine it.

Be careful not to let the village staff bully you into accepting a low price for your unit. Conversely, don't set too high a price or your unit could sit on the market for many months. There is actually quite an art to setting your sale price, and I discuss this in detail in the bonus chapter you can find in the members' section of our website.

---

### A resident's story...

Vivienne lived with her husband in a retirement village on the Sunshine Coast operated by a not-for-profit organisation. Her husband passed away and after 16 years in the complex she decided to sell and move interstate to be closer to family. Having been in residence for such a long period of time, she should have experienced good capital growth and left the complex well in front financially. Unfortunately the village operators sold her unit for quite a low price (only 10 per cent above her original purchase price). Their reason? 'We want to keep prices low so that locals can afford to live here'!

---

# Moving the resident

Some contracts give a village operator the power to move a resident from an ILU or low-care unit into a higher care unit, such as an aged care facility, in the event that they think you need more assistance than you can access in your unit. The clause essentially states that if the village operator thinks you need higher care they can appoint a doctor or similar assessor to evaluate your situation. If the assessor believes you need higher care, the village operator can give you notice to terminate.

This clause is designed to allow the village manager to move on stubborn residents who clearly need constant higher care that cannot be supplied to their unit. The clause may also be needed for residents suffering from Alzheimer's disease or dementia.

However, the village operator could conceivably apply this power maliciously to residents they would like to see removed from the village. I recommend that you change this clause to stipulate the assessor as a registered doctor who is mutually acceptable to both parties. This will protect your interests and ensure that the assessor is not associated with the village operator.

# Village fee

The village fee or general services charge is determined by the retirement village scheme documents. The amount charged to your lot or unit cannot be negotiated. For some new residents I have managed to negotiate village fee holidays, under which the village operator agrees to pay the fee for the incoming resident for a period of, say, 12 months in order to secure the sale.

Village operators are not permitted to include a profit component in their village fee, although this can be hard to regulate, particularly around any head office charges. Some village operators also offer an option for residents to offset the village fee with a higher exit fee if they are struggling to afford the ongoing payments.

For comparison purposes I use $100 per week as the benchmark village fee, although it may be charged on a monthly basis. If a fee were lower than this—say, $80 per week—I would expect the contract arrangements to feature a high exit fee. Leasehold villages also charge a higher village fee of around $120 to $140 per week because it includes a lease component for the land. The Rent Assistance allowance may offset the lease component of the village fee, if you are eligible for this payment.

Residents are obliged to keep paying the village fee until such time as their unit is resold. This means that if a unit is vacant for six months before it is sold, the departing resident or the resident's estate has to continue paying the village fee over that period of time. Some states are now moving to cap this time period in their legislation, usually to around six weeks or 90 days. This is a good outcome, and you should definitely seek to cap the time liability in your contract if the state legislation doesn't stipulate otherwise. Try to negotiate a cap of at least 60 days.

The cap stipulated in the state retirement villages legislation applies only to registered retirement villages.

## Termination

Occasionally a retirement village or village operator will go broke. It doesn't happen often, but it tends to get such extensive media coverage that people think it is a regular occurrence. Many of my clients are concerned about what would happen to them if their village operator went into liquidation, fearing they would be turfed out into the street. Although this is rarely the case, the repercussions of a failed village operator can nevertheless be severe. Typically a retirement village fails if it is underperforming, meaning the operator is unable to sell vacant units because they are too expensive or in a bad location. In this event, you will likely suffer a loss of capital value on your unit because demand, which drives price growth, simply isn't there. Over the long term this may not be an issue, but distressed villages carry a taint for a considerable period of time before they can recoup any lost reputation.

It should be remembered that the governing document for a resident's occupation is the contract you signed at purchase. Depending on the purchase or occupation scheme used by the village, this document could be a lease, a licence or a residential tenancy agreement.

The key point is that these documents remain in force even if the village operator goes broke. Some contracts will consider an event such as the sale or repossession of the village, or default by the village operator, in the termination section. You should be aware of your rights and check with your solicitor that your interests are protected in these circumstances.

## Names on lease

If you are married or have a partner, make sure you both sign the contract. If the signatory to the contract (a lease or licence) dies and the spouse is not named on the contract, the village can legally eject them.

## Age of spouse

Retirement villages have minimum age restrictions on their residents. The actual age varies from village to village. Leasehold retirement villages are also known as over-50s villages and have a much lower age requirement than registered retirement villages. For most registered retirement villages, the minimum age is 60 or 65 years.

You, or your partner or spouse, must meet the minimum age requirement to be allowed to live in the village. For example, if the minimum age limit is 65, so long as you or your spouse is over 65 and you have written approval from the village operator, you will both be allowed to live in the village (unfortunately this won't apply to your toy boy or young girlfriend!). If only one of you meets the minimum age limit, then make sure your purchase contract allows for the under-age resident to remain in the village in the event that the older partner passes away or moves out to higher care.

## Chapter summary

- The ability of a village operator to control its relationship with a resident is greatest at the time of drafting the purchase or occupation contract, so this is the best time for you to get it right.

- When entering into a property negotiation you should try to be in a position that gives you the best chance of success with the purchase.

- For a property purchase, the strongest possible position for a buyer is to be able to deliver the fastest and cleanest purchase contract to the vendor. This is often not about price. A fast and clean contract means:
  - a short contract settlement period
  - few, if any, conditions that must be met before settlement of the contract (for example, building or pest inspection, approval of finance or the sale of an existing property)
  - few, if any, changes to the contract, particularly if they require rewording or review by the vendor's solicitors.

- Use my Contract Comparison Calculator to work out the impact of different terms and conditions on your financial outcome at exit.

- Popular villages that have a waiting list do not usually negotiate on purchase terms.

- Other negotiating tips include:
  - *Deposit.* Get it as low as possible and make sure it is fully refundable in case either party decides not to proceed.
  - *Purchase price.* The lower the better! Because of the time value of money, it always makes sense to get a discount on the upfront purchase price rather than a reduction on the exit fee when you leave.
  - *Inclusions.* For a new strata-titled freehold property you can negotiate for the developer to throw in significant inclusions such as ducted air conditioning, tiles, carpets and ceiling fans.
  - *Deferred fee.* This fee should be as low as possible or spread over a longer period of time.
  - *Share of capital gain.* Aim for as high a share of the capital gain as possible, with little or no share going to the village owner.

- *Refurbishment costs.* The refurbishment scope should not be at the village owner's discretion and costs should be split between the village owner and the resident in the same proportion as the sharing of any capital gains on resale of the unit.

- *Sales commission.* Avoid contracts that lock you into using the village sales staff to sell your unit on exit, and make sure any marketing costs to be paid are capped.

- *Sale price.* The resale price of the unit should be set by the outgoing residents or their estate in conjunction with the village operator. In the event of a dispute over the sale price, an independent valuation can be sought to determine the price.

- *Moving the resident.* Don't accept any clauses that give this power to the village manager. A base position is for this decision to be contingent on the recommendation of a doctor who is mutually acceptable to both parties.

- *Village fee.* This fee is set and cannot be negotiated. However, you should seek to cap your liability to continue paying this fee after exit if the legislation doesn't stipulate otherwise.

- *Termination.* The governing document for a resident's occupation is the contract signed at purchase. This document remains in force even if the village operator goes broke. Check with the contract conveyancing solicitor that your interests are protected in this situation.

- *Names on lease.* If you are married or have a partner, make sure you both sign the contract.

- *Age of spouse.* If your spouse or partner does not meet the minimum age requirements of the village, ensure that your contract allows them to stay in the event that you pass away or need to move out into higher care.

# PART VI

# Living and leaving

Well done, you have almost made it to the end of the book!

In this last part I will look at some of the issues around moving out of your home into the retirement village, as well as living in the village itself. Then I will wrap up by covering the process of leaving your retirement village, and throw in some useful links and resources to help you on your journey.

# Chapter 18

## The big move!

If you are like most retirees, you have probably lived in the same house for the past few decades and this will be your first move for a very long time! For any house move it is important to be as organised as possible to ensure your move goes efficiently, with as little stress as possible. In this chapter I will share with you some useful tips to help with the process.

## Timing your move

In chapter 17 I outlined how your best negotiating position is achieved by having sold your house, or at least having an unconditional contract. While the ideal scenario is to move out of your existing home straight into your new retirement home, timing this sequence is incredibly hard. You have to find and hold your new home with a deposit or exchanged contract, then sell your existing residence, which may take anywhere from 30 days to 12 months!

Most retirement villages will exchange contracts with you that are conditional on the sale of your home, if you haven't already sold it. The contract settlement period (the period between exchange and settlement) is usually 60 to 90 days to give you enough time in which to sell your home. If your home does not sell within this time frame, the contract is cancelled or falls over, and your new retirement home is released back onto the market. Village sales agents, at their discretion, may extend the settlement period if you are close to selling your home. How far you can stretch the process will depend on the village and the village sales agent. If they have a list of other potential buyers waiting for your contract to fall over, then they are unlikely to allow you to extend. Conversely, if the village is struggling to make sales they will probably extend as many times as you want!

It may happen that you sell your home and, for whatever reason, are unable to move immediately into your retirement village. For example, you may not yet have found the right unit. Realistically it may be only a couple of weeks or months that you are without a residence, but the delay can be quite distressing for some people, particularly those who are older or living on their own. It is not the end of the world, though, and you can make temporary (and often fun!) living arrangements such as:

- staying with friends or family
- house-sitting for other people
- packing the caravan, putting everything else into storage and going travelling
- going overseas for a time (preferably somewhere with a low cost of living, such as central and eastern Europe or Asia)
- renting a property, furnished or unfurnished, for a short term. This could be near your future retirement home or somewhere completely different, such as a beach or rural location, or even somewhere like New Zealand. There are also rental retirement villages around that could be an option. Cheap rental options include caravan parks located in regional areas.

So although this delay in your plans can be unsettling, it can also open up some exciting options.

Assuming your plans are progressing more or less as planned, it is now time to start thinking about the move itself.

## Choosing a removal company

There are a number of things you need to consider when choosing a professional removal company. Price is of course a major determining factor, but you should also check their reputation and the insurance cover and written references they can offer.

## Researching removalists

If you are unable to get references from trusted friends and family, then the Yellow Pages or the internet are the most likely places to search for a removalist. If you prefer a local company to a national one, do not restrict yourself to just the area you are moving from, but also research companies in the area you are moving to.

Get quotes from at least three removal firms, but do not be persuaded by price alone, as a quote over the telephone cannot be relied on. Consider the whole package, as some may offer a special discount, better insurance cover or other additional services. Although one company may appear more expensive on paper, their overall service might turn out to be far cheaper and more satisfactory.

## The quote

Most removal companies will send a sales representative to your home to give you an accurate quote. The cost involved with moving is typically based on the number of hours they expect the job to take, plus any additional services you may wish to have them provide, such as packing or storage. Whatever services you request, be sure you get an accurate quotation based on an agreement of their exact obligation to you. Some companies may charge extra for moving a very large, heavy object such as a piano or a pool table.

Ask about the types of insurance they offer to cover any items lost or damaged during the move, and whether they offer a discount if you choose to book a time slot outside their peak operating times. Make sure they are covered by insurance in the event that any of their staff injure themselves in your home. Also ask what is expected of you on the day of the move.

## Checking credentials

Your safest option is to select a nationally recognised company. A larger firm will be more likely to have an established grievance and complaints procedure, and can usually perform your removal on any date of your choosing. National companies may be more expensive but may provide you with greater peace of mind.

If you want extra reassurance, the most reputable companies will have no objection to providing you with written references from previous satisfied customers.

## Moving

There are ways to make the process of packing and unpacking easier and less stressful. Here are some of the best tips I have found:

- All packing boxes need to be lifted by hand, so never load them with more than 20 kilograms, roughly the weight of a full suitcase.
- Pack heavier items at the bottom of the box.
- If boxes are not full, put extra ballast inside to stop things moving around or the boxes crushing. Bed linen, socks and scarves are ideal for this purpose.
- Don't overpack a box.
- If you have lots of small boxes, they may be quicker to move packed into one larger box.
- Ensure you can close all boxes so they can be sealed flat.
- Wrap each breakable item in newspaper or packing paper.
- Depending on what they contain, don't forget to mark them 'this way up' or 'fragile'.
- Label boxes with what they contain and their room designation, as this will make it much easier to find everything when unpacking at the other end.

### To speed things up at the other end

You will most likely be overwhelmed with boxes once you reach your destination. Most can wait but others that will contain essential everyday items, such as the kettle and tea bags! Make sure you can find essential items quickly by labelling these boxes 'load last, unload first'.

### Furniture and larger appliances

Draw up a plan of your new home, mark out exactly where each piece of furniture or large appliance is going to be placed, and give a copy to the removalists. This saves them time, as they will not need to ask you where you want each item to be set down.

## Keep a small set of tools with you

During the process of unpacking, you may find that nuts and screws have fallen off items or components have separated from each other. Keep a small set of tools handy to rectify this.

## Beds first

Your moving day will have been long and exhausting. Besides getting the tea and coffee happening, make sure your bed is assembled and made as soon as you reach your new home. The rest of the house can wait!

---

### *More handy moving tips*

Some more tips to remember:

- Moving day is about moving, not packing. Make sure the packing is all done in the days leading up to the move.

- Get everything moved to the new location before you start to unpack.

- One large, expensive removal van will make for a far quicker, less stressful move than 20 or so trips using cars or a smaller van.

- You need fewer helpers for packing than for moving.

- The earlier in the day you start on moving day the quicker it will be completed, as there will be less traffic on the roads.

- In managing your time schedule, remember that it generally takes three to four times longer to pack a removal van than to unpack it.

- Look on packing and moving as a sort of military exercise in which everyone has a role to play and knows what is expected of them.

---

## Exit checklist

Careful organisation and forward planning can minimise the stress of moving house. Use the moving house checklist (see appendix D on p. 229) and the change of address checklist (see appendix E on p. 233) to guide you through the six weeks leading up to moving day.

## Chapter summary

- Ideally you will move straight from your sold house to your new retirement home. In reality, you cannot always depend on this timing and you may need to consider temporary living arrangements, such as staying with friends or family, house-sitting, travelling or renting short term, before moving into your new home. Although this delay can be unsettling, it can also open up exciting opportunities.

- When choosing a professional removal company there are a number of things you will need to consider.

- If you are unable to get references from trusted friends and family, then the Yellow Pages or the internet are the most likely places to search.

- If you prefer a local company to a national one, do not restrict yourself to the area you are moving from, but also check out companies in the area you are moving to.

- Your safest option is to select a nationally recognised company. It may be more expensive but is likely to give you more peace of mind.

- The removalist's cost is typically based on the number of hours they expect the job to take, plus any additional services such as packing or storage.

- Packing should be done in the days leading up to moving day.

- Draw up a plan of where each item of furniture and appliance will be placed and give a copy to the movers.

- Clearly label all boxes, including those containing essential everyday items, identifying their room designation at destination.

- Use the moving house checklist (see appendix D on p. 229) and change of address checklist (see appendix E on p. 233) to guide you through the weeks leading up to moving day.

# Chapter 19

## Assimilating into village life

If you haven't previously lived in a community environment such as a townhouse or apartment complex, then it is likely that living in a retirement community is going to take some getting used to! Not only is your house and yard smaller than a suburban home's but you will also be living in closer proximity to your neighbours. The good thing is that everyone else is like you! No more noisy neighbours with screaming kids or leaf blowers, just the company of like-minded retirees who want the same things out of life that you do. Do you value your privacy? Fine. Many others in the community do as well. Not everyone wants to spend their time socialising at the barbecue, on outings or on the dinner party circuit.

You do not need to fear community living. All it takes is common sense and a little consideration for others. Sure, there may be people living in the complex you don't get along with. Some may irritate you. This is not unusual. But the feedback I receive from retirement village residents is that the positives of community living greatly outweigh the negatives.

## Getting to know your neighbours

For the first few weeks you will probably be fully taken up with the many tasks involved in getting your new home to feel like home. It is important to re-establish old routines as quickly as possible. However, it is also important not to neglect your social life.

It can be hard simply to approach people you don't know and introduce yourself, especially when it comes to new neighbours. But remember, you are going to be part of a new community and although you may not end up forging strong friendships there, you

177

will begin to feel more settled and at home once you are able to share some neighbourly conversations.

You probably won't need to knock on your neighbours' doors to introduce yourself—you will find that most residents will come and introduce themselves to you in the first instance. During your normal daily activities you will cross paths with other residents from time to time, which will provide opportunities to chat and to get to know each other a little better. Many retirement villages also run a monthly welcome event for new residents. One of the major attractions of a retirement village is the instant social network that the facility provides its residents, so you won't find it too hard to make new friends. It also makes sense to get out and about in the local community to familiarise yourself with what is going on locally, taking a break from the chores at home!

## Residents' committees

The operator is obliged to seek the consent of the village residents before taking certain measures. Consent is sought through the village residents' committee (in a strata-titled freehold village this is the body corporate or owners corporation committee), which is an elected body of residents who represent the interests of the residents. As a resident, you can stand for election to one of the office positions, such as chairperson, treasurer or secretary. You are not compelled to become involved in the committee; however, taking an interest is a good idea if you want to have a say in how the village is operated. Village committees have significant decision-making power and have even been known to turn rogue and sack operators, although this is typically only in extreme cases.

## Village rules

Retirement villages are not required to have rules, although many do. Any formal set of rules should be attached to your purchase contract. The village rules are designed to protect the interests of all the residents and include matters such as pets, entertaining, use of public areas and facilities, and visitor restrictions. It is important to review the village rules as part of your pre-purchase due diligence before signing the contract, to make sure that you have no problems with the kind of restrictions imposed. For example, some village rules will stipulate how long visitors can stay with you, and will allow visitors only if you are also staying at the unit.

## Disputes

It is quite unusual for a resident and a village operator to be unable to resolve any disputes between them. Retirement village operators are running a business and want to see happy customers. They will generally want to engage with you and address any concerns you have. Registered retirement villages should have a formal, written dispute resolution procedure. In the event that you are unable to resolve your differences, however, there is an established path for you to take to seek a settlement.

Your state's department of consumer affairs or fair trading, which administers the retirement villages legislation, also has tribunals that resolve disputes between retirement village operators and residents. Check their website or contact them directly to find out how to lodge a dispute. Lodging a dispute is a serious matter, and the tribunal will want to see that you have exhausted every avenue to resolve your concerns. For more information about the tribunals in your state, see the links and resources in chapter 20.

## Sustainability

Sustainability is the practice of responsible use of resources (such as water, electricity, gas) so as to meet both our own current needs and those of future generations. Sustainability is central to the climate change and carbon emissions debate, as it seeks to reduce the impact or footprint of our lives on the environment.

But what does this have to do with you?

The housing industry in Australia has generally been extremely progressive in developing and managing buildings to world best-practice environmental standards. This means that buildings are designed, built and/or managed to:

- operate efficiently with little or no waste

- reduce wasteful use of resources such as water and power
- recycle materials that can be reused
- improve the quality of the building for tenants or residents.

Unfortunately the retirement living sector has been slow to adopt similar initiatives, and most villages today are inefficiently built and wasteful in their use of energy, and do not promote the use of green initiatives such as water tanks, water recycling or energy-efficient construction techniques. My challenge to you is to organise and motivate your fellow residents to make your own unit and village complex environmentally friendly!

Here are some suggestions to get you started:

- *Step 1: measure.* Speak with your local water and electricity suppliers to find out how you can start measuring your usage. This could involve having metering devices installed or simply collating individual usage data from sources such as rates notices or electricity invoices. Also speak with your local rubbish removalist to measure your waste and recycling. Plot your data into a monthly or quarterly chart so you can compare past and current data to identify improvements.

- *Step 2: bring in the experts.* Local councils, state governments and even the resource providers themselves will often provide free expert audits of your environmental efficiency. Organise for an audit and feedback on how you can reduce your resource use and then implement their recommendations. Many large property companies such as Lend Lease, GPT, Mirvac, Stockland and Jones Lang LaSalle now employ specialists to advise on building sustainability matters. These people are very passionate about their work and more than happy to share ideas and suggestions with you through email or over a cup of coffee.

- *Step 3: plan your initiatives.* Make a list of those things you can change. This list should include the recommendations put forward by the experts in step 2, plus any ideas you have derived from your own research. Think big! There are many government grants and programs you can access to fund your initiatives. Also speak with your local council about sponsoring some of your initiatives, as they may have grant money available.

Here are some project suggestions to get you started:

- energy-efficient lighting throughout the complex
- movement sensor lighting in public areas
- timed, manual air conditioning switches in central activity areas such as clubhouses
- water tank for each unit and the clubhouse to capture rainfall for use in flushing toilets or watering the grounds
- waterless or water-efficient urinals in the men's toilets
- insulation in the roof cavities of each unit and the central facility
- solar hot-water units for each unit and/or the central facility
- solar panels on the roof of your central facilities to power your services and sell power back to the grid
- glazing, shades or awnings, tree planting or similar solutions in areas of the village that suffer from the harsh western sun
- recycling paper, cardboard, plastics and glass from the rubbish
- recycling kitchen and green waste into centrally located compost bins to be used on the village gardens (or even sold outside the village to local gardeners)
- planting native and water-efficient shrubs around the complex
- community food gardens in public spaces. Some large complexes spend a small fortune each year on gardeners — why not turn these expensive garden beds into fruit and vegetable gardens to supplement residents' food budgets?

Of course, much of this work will need to be coordinated through your residents' or owners corporation committee as it affects the whole village. Why not appoint a subcommittee of passionate residents to drive the sustainability project and report back to the main committee?

Although many of these projects will require expenditure, you can access local council, state or federal government grants to carry out the work. Projects that need to be financed from the village sinking funds may actually have a payback period, whereby the money spent on the project is returned over a period of time through lower operating costs. You may also get funding from the village owner.

## Keeping active

The number of retirees I meet who complain of being bored amazes me! There is simply no excuse for this. Retirees can bring a wealth of skills, experience and time to almost any endeavour and have no reason to sit at home feeling bored.

Need some ideas? Here are a few suggestions for you and your retirement village community:

- Harness the creative talents of your fellow residents and book a regular stand at your local weekend market to sell your arts, crafts, photographs, baking and second-hand items. The creator/ supplier sets the price for each item, with a 10 to 20 per cent commission on sales going back into the kitty to pay for the stall and transport expenses. Put a photo and brief bio of the resident beside the item, as this connects the buyer to the producer.

- If you find you have passionate and talented cooks in your complex, compile a collection of their favourite recipes and reproduce them in a booklet or calendar, which could be sold at the market or used as gifts for families and friends. Your village operator may even contribute funds for this activity, as the publication would be a great advertisement for the complex.

- Start a communal fruit and vegetable garden. Many retirement complexes have a lot of public spaces filled with lawns or garden beds. There may even be an adjoining vacant block tipped for future development or adjacent parklands owned by the local council. Get these areas producing food that can be consumed by the residents, sold at the local farmers' market for cash or donated to the needy. Even fences can be productive when covered with creeping vine plants such as passionfruit, grapes, beans, peas or chokos.

- Run monthly or annual gardening competitions among the residents. Get a sponsored prize from your local garden, nursery or hardware shop.

- Contact other retirement villages in the area and arrange get-togethers for bowls, gardening and arts/crafts competitions, barbecues or joint outings.

- Run an annual garage sale for all residents to get rid of things they no longer need. Such an event could be a great story for the local media to cover.

- Start a getaway club and organise monthly overnight trips to nearby destinations. Tours, hotels, motels and restaurants are often very quiet during the week and busy on weekends. If you can plan your trips between Mondays and Wednesdays you should be able to negotiate substantial discounts.

- Find a worthy charity for the entire village to sponsor and run fundraising activities.

Now here are some suggestions for you personally:

- Join a local club such as Rotary, Lions, Probus, Zonta, the Coast Guard, or, if you are interested in business, the local chamber of commerce. Many of these organisations target retirees and feature social activities as well as community service.

- Join a local golf, fishing, boating, bowls or hiking club.

- Get involved in charity work with local special schools or Landcare projects.

- Get involved in your community. This is where you will be living for the foreseeable future, so have your say in how things are run. Go to council meetings and lobby your local representatives for the changes you think will make your community a better place to live.

- Start a small business. You have a wealth of experience and talent that could no doubt be applied to earning you some cash.

- Get a part-time job. Many businesses appreciate the skills and integrity of seniors who are not looking for a career but would like to do a few days work for some extra cash and to keep active and social.

- Get connected. If you haven't already done so, buy a computer and get connected to the internet (it must be broadband, not dial-up). There are many free courses that will get you set up and operating in no time. Check your local TAFE, library or even the store where you bought your computer to find out about these courses. Or simply ask the nearest 12 year old for help! Getting connected to the internet for the first time is like opening a door to the entire world. It also puts you in closer touch with family and friends, especially grandchildren, who communicate primarily through electronic media.

- Start a new hobby. Many of us give up our hobbies because of family or work commitments; now is the time to dust off those dreams of train sets, kites, model planes, coin collecting, fly tying, cake decorating, sewing, fishing, getting your pilot's licence or buying a motorbike.

- Research your family tree. There are terrific resources now available to assist people with researching their family tree. Dry old charts and diagrams can now be augmented with photos, medals, birth certificates and headstone rubbings. Your research may also take you on fact-finding missions overseas!

- Travel! Getting out and about to see the world can be done very cheaply now — don't think you are stuck with the traditional coach tours or cruises with other old people. You can take extended trips to countries such as Thailand, Malaysia or Vietnam very cheaply. South America and some parts of eastern Europe are also very cheap to get around and stay in.

- Take classes. Learn a language or a musical instrument, or sign up for art classes; go back to school and get another degree.

- How about dating? If you are single, get back into the market!

- Take up some exercise. Every health practitioner will tell you that you 'use it or lose it'. Find some physical activities you enjoy and go for it. Don't make the mistake of choosing just one exercise, such as walking. Try to find a few different activities that you enjoy and do them each week, as this will prevent you from becoming bored with the same exercise routine.

- Shop for bargains! You now have more time to research and go out of your way for better prices.

The important thing is to follow your passions or interests. This is your time now, and you should have a go at all of those things you enjoyed doing in the past or have put off doing for lack of time or opportunity.

---

### Getting connected

Telstra Connected Seniors is a tailored program created to help older Australians learn more about technology. It offers individual self-teach guides and fun interactive workshops. It also provides eligible community groups with funding opportunities to run successful training courses around technology. If you want to stay in touch with your children and grandchildren, you have to embrace new technology and make the internet and email a part of your daily life.

---

# Filling the void

Man is so made that he can only find relaxation from one kind of labor by taking up another.

Anatole France
French poet and novelist (1844–1924)

You have worked hard for more than 40 years, dreaming of the day when you won't have to get up to an alarm clock and can set your own agenda, a slave to the system no longer. But is retirement really that wonderful? Quitting the rat race of income-driven work removes many stresses from your life but replaces them with a big, gaping void — the sea of endless opportunity.

In the absence of deadlines, reports, performance appraisals, budgets and co-workers, your thoughts will naturally turn to a question you last worried over in your late teens — what am I going to do with my life?

It is natural that doubts will fill your mind. As you sit on your front step sipping your tea in the morning sunshine, watching your neighbours rushing off to catch the bus for work, you may even feel guilty. Being productive is so highly valued by our society that for many people retirement leads to feelings of purposelessness, which can lower self-esteem. One of the commonly felt experiences soon after retirement is boredom. All these feelings are normal. You are not the first person to retire and experience the emotional highs and lows of this life-changing event.

The truth is that, having worked most of your life, you deserve the opportunity to retire. Your challenge is how to enjoy it without experiencing the sense of purposelessness and depression that is felt by many retirees.

Some people equate retirement with the freedom to do what I want'. For many, however, it also means limitations, a sense of loss, financial worries, and concerns about how to stay healthy and leave family members unburdened. The very freedom that creates joy for many can for others be imprisoning, both emotionally and socially. Without the routine of work, people lose structure, social interactions, and a sense of purpose and professional identity, as well as income. For some, too much time on their hands leads to anxiety and depression. The time to think allows for unresolved conflicts of the past to surface.

For couples, changes occur in the balance of chores, roles and power. The extra time together can be experienced as wonderful or smothering. Don't expect simply to replace those eight hours apart with 12 hours of meaningful togetherness. Look for common interests and things you both like to do. Try making dates with your partner to enjoy quality time together. Make a list of things you like to do and have your partner do the same, then take turns at doing what your partner enjoys. Balance time alone with time together.

Structure your time. Plan each day to include reading, fun and relaxation—mental and physical activities. Get up at the same time each day and plan to exercise, walk, go to a club, do yoga or meditation, or go out for a meal. Plan your day to include things that are good for you physically, emotionally and spiritually.

Walk instead of driving. Learn to enjoy the journey as much as the destination. It takes more time to get there and is good exercise.

Decide how you want to be remembered and try to live up to that right now!

---

### Ageing entrepreneurs

Did you know that rates of entrepreneurship are 50 per cent higher among people aged between 55 and 64 than people between 20 and 34? According to the Kauffman Foundation <www.kauffman.org>, rates of entrepreneurship among people aged 55 to 64 have generally been trending up since 2007, whereas rates for the younger group have stayed relatively flat.

It appears there are various reasons for this. Often people aged 50+ who are made redundant from a middle or senior management job struggle to find gainful employment. In this event, some find they have no other option than to start their own business. Older retirees may simply find retirement boring, and they know they have all these great skills sitting there unutilised.

Attitudes towards retirement are changing. Some people no longer dream of a life of leisure sitting around a retirement village, golfing, fishing or whatever. People can and do want to stay productive as long as possible.

Advances in technology and Australia's relatively low rate of unemployment mean more organisations are amenable to their workers telecommuting or contracting. This type of work solution, which has really never been available before, allows retirees to become productive once again on their own terms! No more 9 to 5 daily commute on inefficient public transport—productive retirees of today can work from home or set their own flexible office hours.

This may be what retirement will ultimately become—simply the opportunity to set your own work schedule while doing something you enjoy.

---

## Post-retirement anxiety and depression

Talk to friends and family about what you are going through and seek professional help if necessary.

## *Depression and anxiety in older people*

beyondblue's research shows that it is a commonly held view among people of all ages—including older people—that as we reach the latter stages of our lives, it is normal for people to become depressed.

Additionally, older people particularly are still more likely to consider depression to be a weakness of character and do not view it in the context of a health problem, so they often don't talk about how they're feeling or seek help early.

There are risk factors right across the lifespan which can increase a person's risk of developing depression at a particular stage of life. In later life the following can increase people's chances of developing depression because of:

- an increase in physical health problems or conditions (for example heart disease, stroke, Alzheimer's disease)
- chronic pain
- side-effects from medications
- losses (relationships, independence, work and income, self-worth, mobility and flexibility)
- social isolation
- significant change in living arrangements (for example moving from an independent to care setting)
- admission to hospital
- particular anniversaries and the memories they evoke.

The most important message about depression and older people is that depression is *not* a normal part of ageing. Depression is a common health problem and, with the right treatment, most people recover.

Source: © beyondblue—the national depression initiative <www.beyondblue.org.au>.

How do you know when you are depressed? Symptoms include:

- persistent sad or anxious moods
- feelings of emptiness, hopelessness or pessimism
- loss of pleasure or interest in ordinary activities

- sleep problems (too much or too little)
- loss of appetite or a tendency to overeat
- reduced energy
- restlessness or irritability
- difficulty in concentrating, remembering or making decisions
- inappropriate feelings of guilt
- thoughts of death or suicide.

If you recognise these depression symptoms, please see your doctor.

## Leaving the village

If you have done your research and sought good advice, then your stay in a retirement community should be long and pleasant. There will come a time, however, when you have to leave.

Some people leave a retirement village because they are not happy there (for whatever reason) or they want to move closer to family. More likely, they move on to a higher care facility or they pass away. The practical process for leaving a retirement community is outlined in your purchase contract and the state retirement villages legislation, and typically involves a notice period after some form of written notification to the village operator.

Following formal notification of departure, the resident or the resident's estate is required to return the unit to the village operator within a certain time frame, usually around 30 days, with what is known as vacant possession. Vacant possession simply means that the unit has been cleared of all personal items and cleaned, and the keys handed over to the village operator.

Table 19.1 (overleaf) outlines the responsibilities of the resident or the resident's estate during the typical leaving process.

Table 19.1: leaving the village

| Order | Event |
|---|---|
| 1 | Provide written notice to the village operator. |
| 2 | Provide the village operator with vacant possession of the unit. |
| 3 | Agree on a resale value with the village operator. |
| 4 | Agree on the scope and cost of unit refurbishment. |
| 5 | Complete the refurbishment and reinstatement of the unit. |
| 6 | Resell the unit. |
| 7 | Receive the exit entitlement, less the deferred fee, the village operator's share of any capital gains, and any other outstanding fees and charges. |

# Setting a sale price

The sale price of your unit is negotiated between you or your estate and the village operator. The price is typically set by looking at past sales of similar units in your village or in adjacent retirement villages.

If you are unable to agree on a sale price with the village operator, then a valuer is appointed to determine a price. The cost of this valuation may be split equally between you and the village operator, completely covered by you or split in the same proportion as the sharing of capital gains, depending on the wording of your original purchase contract.

The independent valuation then becomes the sale price. You need to be aware that if you decide to accept a sale price that is lower than either the valuation or the sale price previously agreed with the village operator, then most contracts will allow for the operator to base all of the exit fees and charges on the valuation or agreed price, rather than the actual sale price. For example, if you and the village operator agreed on a sale price of $400 000 but you ended up accepting an offer of $385 000, then the village operator would base the deferred fee and sharing of capital gains calculations on the agreed price of $400 000, not the accepted price of $385 000. In the event that the village operator accepts the lower price, however, then the fee calculations are based on the lower accepted price and not the original agreed price. I know this sounds confusing, but the point is to make sure the village operator agrees to formally accept the lower price and to base your exit fee calculations on the lower value.

As discussed in chapter 11, most purchase contracts also contain a provision for you to make up any capital loss on the sale of your unit to the village operator in the event that your unit sells for less than your original purchase price. For example, if your original ingoing contribution was $250 000 and you resold your unit at a later date for $235 000, you would have to pay the difference of $15 000 ($250 000–$235 000) to the village operator.

## Selling your unit

Once the formal notification of departure has been received, the village operator begins organising the refurbishment and resale of the unit around the resident's moving timetable. The refurbishment may take anywhere from one to three months once the unit has been vacated, although the operator should begin marketing the unit for sale immediately.

It is important to stay in constant contact with the village operator over this time to make sure that refurbishment work, and sales and marketing activities are actively progressed. Do not simply get on with your life assuming that the operator is working hard to get your unit back on the market and resold. I have heard far too many stories of units sitting vacant for months and months, tying up cash that could be better used elsewhere. You may also find that a delayed sale results in a higher deferred management fee, as this charge continues to accrue until the unit is resold. It is an unfortunate fact that the quality of sales and marketing agents of retirement complexes is woeful. Many lack basic real estate qualifications (in some states you do not even have to be a registered real estate agent to sell retirement village units) and sales training, which may be an advantage when you are buying a retirement home, but is certainly a disadvantage when you are trying to sell.

As a minimum, then, I suggest that you take the following precautions:

- Ask the village sales agent to provide you with a weekly update on the progress of the refurbishment and marketing activities. If they are unable to provide this, you need to take the initiative and contact them regularly yourself.

- Check the village website to make sure your unit is featured for sale. Does the online feature include basic information such as photographs, an internal floor layout and pricing?

- Make sure the marketing photographs of the unit are of sufficient quality.

- Get your friends to contact the sales agent as prospective buyers to see what they are saying about the unit (you would be horrified by some of the comments made).

- Ask to see a marketing plan.

- Check the pricing of comparable retirement units and residential properties in the same general area to assess the reasonableness of your asking price—don't just rely on the sales agent's advice.

Once your unit has been resold and settled, the operator will receive the sale money and subtract the relevant fees. The remaining funds will then be returned to you or your estate. The operator should also supply you with a reconciliation of the fees and charges that have been subtracted, and you should check each item closely.

## Chapter summary

- It is not compulsory for a retirement village to have fixed rules, although many do. A formal set of rules should be attached to your purchase contract.

- The village operator is obliged to seek the consent of the residents before undertaking certain actions or measures. This consent is gained through the village residents' committee, which is an elected body of residents who represent the residents.

- Sustainability is the practice of responsible use of resources (such as water, electricity, gas) so as to meet both our own current needs and those of future generations. This means that buildings are designed, built and/or managed to:

- – operate efficiently with little or no waste
- – reduce water and power usage
- – recycle materials that can be reused
- – improve the quality of the buildings for residents.

- It is important to keep active and follow your passions or interests in your retirement. This is your time and you should have a go at all those things you once enjoyed or have put off for lack of time or opportunity.

- Post-retirement depression is common. You should plan your retirement to keep active and healthy. If you recognise the signs of depression, seek medical help.

- The process when leaving a retirement community is outlined in the purchase contract and the state retirement villages legislation. It typically begins with you providing formal, written notification to the village operator.

- Do not assume that the operator is working hard to get your unit back on the market and resold. Check on progress regularly!

# Chapter 20
## Links and resources

This chapter contains a list of state and territory specific useful resources to assist with your retirement home research, as well as some general information about retirement and ageing. There is a wealth of resources and information available today on the internet, so I would strongly encourage you to get connected if you are not already online. Phoning around for information and advice can be time consuming, expensive and ultimately ineffective. If you don't like reading on a computer screen, you can always print the appropriate pages on paper and read them in the traditional way with a highlighter and pencil poised!

## Queensland
### Legislation
*Retirement Villages Act 1999*

*Retirement Villages Amendment Act 1999*

*Retirement Villages Regulation 2000*

### Administration
**Queensland Office of Fair Trading**

<www.fairtrading.qld.gov.au>

Phone: 13 1304

This regulatory body administers the state's legislation covering retirement villages, property transactions and real estate agent licensing and behaviour. They are your first point of contact if you have concerns or questions regarding your real estate agent or a retirement village operator.

## Disputes
### Queensland Civil and Administrative Tribunal

<www.qcat.qld.gov.au>

Phone: 1300 753 228

# New South Wales
## Legislation

*Retirement Villages Act 1999*

*Retirement Villages Regulation 2000*

*Retirement Villages Transitional Regulation 2000*

*Retirement Villages Amendment Act 2008*

*Retirement Villages Regulation 2009*

## Administration
### NSW Office of Fair Trading

<www.fairtrading.nsw.gov.au>

This regulatory body administers the state's legislation covering retirement villages, property transactions and real estate agent licensing and behaviour. It is your first point of contact if you have concerns or questions regarding your real estate agent or a retirement village operator.

## Disputes
### NSW Consumer, Trader and Tenancy Tribunal

<www.cttt.nsw.gov.au>

Phone: 1300 135 399

# Other
## Council on the Ageing (NSW)

<www.cotansw.com.au>

Level 6, 280 Pitt Street

Sydney NSW 2000

Free call: 1800 449 102

COTA NSW works with government, business, the media and the wider community to represent the aspirations and concerns of seniors.

## Law Society NSW

Phone: 1800 422 713

Contact the Law Society for referrals to solicitors in your area who specialise in retirement village purchase contracts.

## Retirement Village Residents Association (NSW)

<www.rvra.org.au>

# Victoria
## Legislation

*Retirement Villages Act 1986*

*Retirement Villages (Records & Notices) Regulations 2005*

*Retirement Villages (Contractual Arrangements) Regulations 2006*

*Estate Agents (Retirement Villages) Regulations 2006*

# Administration
## Consumer Affairs Victoria

<www.www.consumer.vic.gov.au>

GPO Box 123

Melbourne VIC 3001

This regulatory body administers the state's legislation covering retirement villages, property transactions and real estate agent licensing and behaviour. It is your first point of contact if you have concerns or questions regarding your real estate agent or a retirement village operator.

**Victorian Consumer & Business Centre**

113 Exhibition Street

Melbourne VIC 3000

Phone: 1300 558 181

Email: consumer@justice.vic.gov.au

## Disputes
**VIC Civil and Administrative Tribunal**

<www.vcat.vic.gov.au>

## Other
**Retirement Village Residents Association (VIC)**

PO Box 4316

Knox City Centre VIC 3152

Phone: (03) 9015 8402

# Australian Capital Territory
## Legislation
*Fair Trading Act 1992*

*Retirement Villages Industry Code of Practice 1999*

## Administration
**ACT Office of Regulatory Services**

<www.ors.act.gov.au>

This regulatory body administers the territory's legislation covering retirement villages, property transactions and real estate agent licensing and behaviour. It is your first point of contact if you have concerns or questions regarding your real estate agent or a retirement village operator.

**Office of Regulatory Services**

Callam Offices, Easty Street (off Launceston Street)

Phillip, ACT

GPO Box 158

Canberra ACT 2601

Phone: (02) 6207 0400

Fax: (02) 6207 0538

# Tasmania
## Legislation
*Retirement Villages Act 2004*

## Administration
### Consumer Affairs and Fair Trading

<www.consumer.tas.gov.au>

Level 3, 15 Murray Street

Hobart TAS 7000

Phone: 1300 654 499

Fax: (03) 6233 4882

Email: consumer.affairs@justice.tas.gov.au

This regulatory body administers the state's legislation covering retirement villages, property transactions and real estate agent licensing and behaviour. It is your first point of contact if you have concerns or questions regarding your real estate agent or a retirement village operator.

# South Australia
## Legislation
*Retirement Villages Act 1987*

*Retirement Villages (Miscellaneous) Amendment Act 2001*

*Retirement Villages (Miscellaneous) Amendment Act 2005*

*Retirement Villages Regulations*

# Administration
## Office for the Ageing

<www.ageing.sa.gov.au>

Level 4, South West Riverside Centre

North Terrace

Adelaide SA 5000

Phone: (08) 8207 0522

Fax: (08) 8207 0555

Email: ofta@saugov.sa.gov.au

The Office for the Ageing is responsible for policy advice, development, funding and implementation of programs and services for older people in South Australia, including administration of the retirement villages legislation.

## Consumer and Business Services

<www.ocba.sa.gov.au>

This regulatory body administers the state's legislation covering property transactions and real estate agent licensing and behaviour. This department should be your first point of contact if you have concerns or questions regarding your real estate agent.

# Western Australia
## Legislation
*Retirement Villages Act 1992*

*Retirement Villages Regulations 19992*

*Code of Fair Practice for Retirement Villages*

## Administration

**Department of Commerce (Consumer Protection)**

<www.commerce.wa.gov.au>

Department of Commerce

The Forrest Centre, 221 St Georges Terrace

Perth WA 6000

Phone: 1300 136 237

This regulatory body administers the state's legislation covering retirement villages, property transactions and real estate agent licensing and behaviour. It is your first point of contact if you have concerns or questions regarding your real estate agent or a retirement village operator.

# Northern Territory
## Legislation

*Retirement Villages Act 1995*

*Retirement Villages Regulations 1995*

## Administration

**NT Consumer Affairs**

<www.nt.gov.au/justice/consaffairs>

This regulatory body administers the territory's legislation covering retirement villages, property transactions and real estate agent licensing and behaviour. It is your first point of contact if you have concerns or questions regarding your real estate agent or a retirement village operator.

# Other resources
## Find My Retirement Home

Our website contains a members' section that you can access for free — simply click the 'Members' link and enter your username and password, as noted in the introduction of this book. On the website you will find the following:

- a bonus chapter, 'Selling your home', that provides information to help you with:
  - selecting and appointing a real estate agent
  - types of appointment
  - driving your real estate agent
  - commissions and fees
  - methods of sale, explaining which one is best and most appropriate for your home
  - presenting your home for buyer inspections
  - how to fund presentation work to bring your home up to a saleable condition
- a members' forum where you can ask questions, compare notes and share experiences with other retirees going through the same process
- the Contract Comparison Calculator
- downloadable copies of the worksheets included in the back of this book
- free webinars
- video and audio recordings about buying and living in retirement homes
- a question-and-answer facility where your questions can be put to retirement home experts
- special discounts and deals.

The Find My Retirement Home members' website is a free and an essential tool for your retirement home research.

## Aged care brokers

If either you or your ageing relatives need help in sourcing an aged care facility, you should contact an aged care broker. Essentially, brokers provide a placement service: they will help you find a place in an appropriate aged care facility. A good broker will also help negotiate the financial aspects of moving a loved one into aged care, although it is always worth contacting your financial adviser for advice too.

**Millennium Aged Care Placement Consultants**

<www.millenniumagedcare.com.au>

Phone: 1300 755 702

**Future Care Solutions**

<www.futurecaresolutions.com.au>

Phone: (07) 3881 0616

## Capital growth forecasts

<www.residex.com.au>

<www.homepriceguide.com.au>

<www.myrpdata.com.au>

<www.onthehouse.com.au>

Use these sites to order analysis reports on the postcode or area where you are looking to buy your retirement home. The reports can provide you with historical capital growth for a particular area and, in some cases, forward estimates on future capital growth prospects.

## Home inspections/handovers

**Archicentre**

<www.archicentre.com.au>

530 Glenferrie Road

Hawthorn VIC 3122

Archicentre is the building advisory service of the Australian Institute of Architects, offering service and advice to homebuyers, new home builders and renovators. Archicentre has more than 900 architects, available in nearly every suburb and region across Australia, to perform prompt and professional services. With its head office in Victoria, it has branch offices in most states of Australia.

Archicentre offers free technical advice to thousands of homebuyers across the country through a range of property inspections, the Architect's Advice helpline, homebuyer seminars run in most states, and technical sheets on house faults and design issues.

**Handovers.com**

<www.handovers.com>

Phone: 1300 131 041

Handovers specialises in doing Practical Completion or handover inspections with builders on behalf of buyers. If you want the assurance of a professional inspection of your newly constructed property, this is a great service.

# Moving day

**The Finishing Touch**

<www.ftouch.com.au>

Phone: 1300 367 269

Having handled more than 50 000 moves since 1994, The Finishing Touch offers Australia's most experienced home packing, unpacking, pre-move assist and home organising solution. All Finishing Touch services are provided on a fixed hourly rate and are designed to help you reduce stress, save time and be more organised when moving house.

**Smooth Move Projects**

<www.smoothmoveprojects.com.au>

Phone: 1300 364 003

Smooth Move Projects helps families to transition from their home to aged care and retirement facilities. Smooth Move Projects is a national service provider of aged care services that offers a full and personalised service with the objective of absorbing all of the stresses related to relocation.

# Real estate

## Jenman Group

<www.jenman.com.au>

Real estate agents across Australia passionately hate self-styled consumers' advocate Neil Jenman, which is probably a good reason to check out his books and website! The site offers great consumer resources relating to buying and selling homes. I thoroughly recommend it.

## Real Estate Institute of Australia

<www.reia.com.au>

Members of each state and territory real estate institute are automatically members of the REIA. This site has links to the state and territory real estate institutes. In addition, it offers interesting generic information for consumers. Remember, though, this is a representative body for real estate agents, not consumers.

# Retirement villages

## Retirement Village Association

<www.rva.com.au>

The national association for the owners, operators, developers and others associated with retirement villages in Australia. It is an industry body that administers an accreditation program for retirement villages. It also has a useful directory search function if you want a list of villages in a particular location, although the list will not be exhaustive.

## Retirement Village Residents Association

<www.rvra.org.au>

The Retirement Village Residents Association aims to:

* increase retirement village residents' awareness and understanding of their rights and obligations
* defend and extend the rights of residents in retirement villages

- encourage residents to exercise their rights and to participate in decision making that affects their lives
- encourage and assist residents to form and participate in the functioning of residents' committees
- offer information and advice to prospective residents. RVRA cannot offer legal advice but can direct people to appropriate organisations.
- encourage the development of positive relationships between residents and management.

**Village research websites**

<www.yellowpages.com.au>

<www.seniorlivingonline.com.au>

<www.seniorshousingonline.com.au>

<www.retirementlivingonline.com.au>

<www.itsyourlife.com.au>

<www.villages.com.au>

<www.rva.com.au>

# Seniors

## Australian Government information portal for seniors

<www.seniors.gov.au>

This is the Australian Government's premier source of information for Australians over 50.

## Council of the Ageing

<www.cota.org.au>

GPO Box 1583

Adelaide, SA 5001

Phone: 1800 182 324

Fax: (08) 8232 0433

Email: cota@cotaaustralia.org.au

COTA seeks to promote and protect the interests and wellbeing of all seniors, and is an independent consumer organisation run by and for senior Australians. COTA Australia has individual members and seniors organisation members in all states and territories.

**National Seniors Australia**

<www.nationalseniors.com.au>

Level 18, 215 Adelaide Street

Brisbane QLD 4000

Phone: 1300 765 050

Fax: (07) 3211 9339

Email: general@nationalseniors.com.au

NSA is a not-for-profit, membership-based organisation assisting the over-50s community by providing economic and social benefits and representing seniors' views to government at all levels

# Where to retire

**In Australia**

<www.where2retire.com.au>

This website supports Jill and Owen Weekes' bestselling book *Where to Retire in Australia*. The book is an essential guide for all who need help to figure out where to base their new life after retirement.

**Retiring overseas**

<www.retire-abroad.org>

<www.escapeartist.com>

<ww.boomersabroad.com>

<www.retiring-overseas.com>

<www.shelteroffshore.com>

<www.retireoverseasnow.com>

<www.whyretireinthailand.com>

<www.mm2h.gov.my>

# Chapter 21
## The final word

I think that just about wraps it up! I hope you have enjoyed this book and found some useful ways to save yourself time and money on your retirement journey. You now have all the information you need to make informed decisions concerning your retirement options, and you have the tools to negotiate a great deal on your retirement home purchase.

I also hope I haven't scared you off moving into a retirement community! Retirement villages offer retirees a great lifestyle option, with homes specially built for low maintenance and an instant social network of like-minded people. You need only make sure you do your research and get good advice.

Please sign up for free membership on our website <www.findmyretirementhome.com.au> using the password 'retire'. You can also find us on Facebook under 'Find My Retirement Home', and check out our YouTube channel under 'the Retire Guy'. Make sure you link to these sites, as I regularly post updates about retirement home purchases, and the dates and times of my seminars or other speaking engagements around the country.

If you get stuck, the members' section of our website has a list of the contact details of accountants, financial planners and solicitors around Australia I have trained and certified to help you with your retirement home purchase. Alternatively, you can always call us for a chat on 1300 425 442. Best wishes for a happy retirement!

**Richard Andrews**
**Founder and CEO, Find My Retirement Home**

# Appendix A
# Preference questionnaire

## Location preferences

List the locations where you would like to live in order of preference.
If you have only one preference, leave remainder blank.

| | |
|---|---|
| 1 | |
| 2 | |
| 3 | |

What is important to you in these locations (for example, climate, lifestyle, close to family)?

| |
|---|
| |
| |
| |

What clubs, associations, sporting activities and other attractions are important to you (colour appropriate circle)?

| | Essential | Desirable | Not important |
|---|---|---|---|
| Bowls club | O | O | O |
| Golf club | O | O | O |
| Fishing | O | O | O |
| Swimming club | O | O | O |
| Bridge club | O | O | O |
| Tennis club | O | O | O |
| RSL | O | O | O |
| CWA | O | O | O |

*(Clubs and activities cont'd)*

| | | | |
|---|---|---|---|
| Culture (e.g. theatres, museums) | O | O | O |
| Cinema | O | O | O |
| Rotary | O | O | O |
| Lions | O | O | O |
| Probus | O | O | O |
| Employment opportunities | O | O | O |
| Shopping | O | O | O |
| River | O | O | O |
| Beach | O | O | O |
| Other (please list) | | | |

# Village/community preferences

| | Essential | Desirable | Not important |
|---|---|---|---|
| Small complex (<30 units) | O | O | O |
| Larger complex (>30 units) | O | O | O |
| New property | O | O | O |
| Religious | O | O | O |
| Non-denominational | O | O | O |
| Access to broadband internet | O | O | O |
| Garden/yard | O | O | O |
| Pets | O | O | O |
| Walk to public transport | O | O | O |
| Bowling green | O | O | O |
| Meal service by request | O | O | O |
| Laundry service by request | O | O | O |
| Linen provided | O | O | O |

| | | | |
|---|---|---|---|
| Registered retirement village | O | O | O |
| On-site manager | O | O | O |
| On-site security | O | O | O |
| On-site medical staff | O | O | O |
| Sustainability initiatives (for example, solar power) | O | O | O |
| Other (please list) | | | |

# Financial considerations

Indicate your purchase price range:

Minimum    $

Maximum    $

| | Essential | Desirable | Not important |
|---|---|---|---|
| Weekly fee under $100 | O | O | O |
| Low purchase price | O | O | O |
| Low exit fees | O | O | O |
| Freehold title on property | O | O | O |
| Buy-back guarantee on exit | O | O | O |
| Ability to mortgage property | O | O | O |

# Property preferences

Please select your property preferences from the following table.

| | Essential | Desirable | Not important |
|---|---|---|---|
| New property | O | O | O |
| Freehold or equivalent | O | O | O |
| Detached house/ villa | O | O | O |
| Apartment | O | O | O |
| Townhouse/duplex | O | O | O |
| Studio | O | O | O |
| 1 bedroom | O | O | O |
| 2 bedroom | O | O | O |
| 2 bedroom + study | O | O | O |
| 3 bedroom | O | O | O |
| 1 bathroom | O | O | O |
| 1.5 bathroom | O | O | O |
| 2 bathroom | O | O | O |
| 1 car garage | O | O | O |
| 2 car garage | O | O | O |
| Hardstand for caravan/boat | O | O | O |
| Multi-level | O | O | O |
| Flat, no steps or slopes | O | O | O |
| Air conditioning | O | O | O |
| Patio/outdoor living area | O | O | O |
| Heating | O | O | O |
| Personal distress alarm | O | O | O |
| Security screens/ system | O | O | O |

| High quality finishes | O | O | O |
| Gas kitchen | O | O | O |
| Garden area | O | O | O |

# Health and mobility

List any existing health concerns, which require regular medical attention.

How regularly do you require the services or a doctor or specialist?

| More than once per week | O | Once per month | O |
| Once per fortnight | O | Once every few months | O |

# Appendix B
# Individual village questionnaire

Village:

Date inspected:

| Complex summary | | |
|---|---|---|
| Address | | |
| Postcode | | |
| Telephone | | |
| Website | | |
| Operator/owner | | |
| Registered retirement village | (Y/N) | |
| Accredited retirement village | (Y/N) | |
| Year constructed | | |
| Avg. age of residents | | |
| Avg. time in residence | (years) | |
| Avg. sale time | (months) | |
| No. units in village | | |
| No. vacancies | | |
| Pool | (Y/N) | |
| Club house | (Y/N) | |
| Bowling green | (Y/N) | |
| Pets | (Y/N) | |
| Other | (list) | |
| Community bus | (Y/N) | |

| | | |
|---|---|---|
| Meals | (Y/N) | |
| Higher care services available | (Y/N) | |
| Linen/laundry service | (Y/N) | |
| On-site manager | (Y/N) | |
| Residents committee | (Y/N) | |
| Personal distress alarms | (Y/N) | |
| Security system | (Y/N) | |
| On-site medical staff | (Y/N) | |
| **Preferred unit summary** | | |
| Description | | |
| Internal size (sq. m.) from: | | |
| Studio apartment | | |
| 1 bedroom apartment | | |
| 2 bedroom apartment | | |
| 1 bedroom villa | | |
| 2 bedroom villa | | |
| 2 bedroom + study villa | | |
| 3 bedroom villa | | |
| Air conditioning | (Y/N) | |
| Garden | (Y/N) | |
| Patio/outdoor | (Y/N) | |
| Undercover parking | (number of spaces) | |
| External hardstand for boat/caravan | (Y/N) | |
| Level of finishes | (good/average, etc.) | |
| Views | (Y/N) | |
| Available now? | (Y/N) | |
| Other | | |

| Financial summary | | |
|---|---|---|
| Freehold | (Y/N) | |
| Leasehold | (Y/N) | |
| Loan/lease | (Y/N) | |
| Loan/licence | (Y/N) | |
| Fee cap | (%) | |
| Number of years | | |
| Fee per annum | (%) | |
| DMF on entry/exit | | |
| Capital gain split to complex owner | (%) | |
| Structure flexibility | (Y/N) | |
| Re-sale commission | (%) | |
| Refurbishment charge | ($) | |
| Re-sale guarantee | (Y/N) | |
| General services fee | ($) | |
| Other fees | ($) | |
| Preferred unit price range ($): | | |
| Studio apartment | | |
| 1 bedroom apartment | | |
| 2 bedroom apartment | | |
| 1 bedroom villa | | |
| 2 bedroom villa | | |
| 2 bedroom + study villa | | |
| 2 bedroom villa | | |
| Deposit required | | |
| Settlement period | | |
| Rates | ($) | |
| Body corporate fees | ($) | |

# Appendix C
# Research comparison
# worksheet

In appendix C you can summarise your findings from the individual village questionnaires you filled out in appendix B. On the following pages, compare the different retirement villages you have researched and work out which one suits your specific needs. Enter the shortlisted villages along the top row and record your research results under each village using the data you have sourced for your individual village questionnaires. This worksheet is designed to help you easily compare the various services, facilities, fees and location attributes of your shortlisted communities.

You can also download a version of this worksheet from the members' section of our website at <www.findmyretirementhome. com.au> using the password 'retire'.

| Villages | | | |
|---|---|---|---|
| **Location summary** | | | |
| Suburb | | | |
| Postcode | | | |
| Median unit price ($) | | | |
| Last 12 months capital growth (units) (%) | | | |
| Average capital growth last 10 years (units) (%) | | | |
| Median house price | | | |
| Last 12 months capital growth (houses) (%) | | | |
| Average cap growth last 10 years (houses) (%) | | | |
| Capital growth forecast—10 years (%) | | | |
| **Complex summary** | | | |
| Address | | | |
| Telephone | | | |
| Website | | | |

## Appendix C: Research comparison worksheet

| | | | |
|---|---|---|---|
| Operator/owner | | | |
| Registered retirement village (Y/N) | | | |
| Year constructed | | | |
| Average age of residents | | | |
| Average time in residence | | | |
| Number of units in village | | | |
| Number of vacancies | | | |
| Pool (Y/N) | | | |
| Clubhouse (Y/N) | | | |
| Bowling green (Y/N) | | | |
| Pets (Y/N) | | | |
| Other | | | |
| Community bus (Y/N) | | | |
| Meals (Y/N) | | | |
| Higher care services available (Y/N) | | | |
| Linen/laundry service (Y/N) | | | |
| On-site manager (Y/N) | | | |
| Residents committee (Y/N) | | | |

| | | | | |
|---|---|---|---|---|
| Personal distress alarms | (Y/N) | | | |
| Security system | (Y/N) | | | |
| On-site medical staff | (Y/N) | | | |
| Nearest capital city | | | | |
| Nearest hospital | | | | |
| Nearest international airport | | | | |
| **Distance to (km)** | | | | |
| Medical centre | | | | |
| Hospital | | | | |
| Neighbourhood shopping centre | | | | |
| Golf course | | | | |
| Bowls club | | | | |
| RSL | | | | |
| Other club | | | | |
| Bus | | | | |
| Train | | | | |
| Airport | | | | |
| Beach/river | | | | |

| | | | |
|---|---|---|---|
| Public swimming pool | | | |
| Other | | | |
| **Clubs and associations in district** | | | |
| Lions | (Y/N) | | |
| Rotary | (Y/N) | | |
| Other | | | |
| **Preferred unit summary** | | | |
| Description | | | |
| Internal size (sq m) from: | | | |
| Studio apartment | | | |
| 1 bedroom apartment | | | |
| 2 bedroom apartment | | | |
| 1 bedroom villa | | | |
| 2 bedroom villa | | | |
| 3 bedroom villa | | | |
| Air conditioning | (Y/N) | | |
| Garden | | | |
| Patio/outdoor | | | |

| | | | |
|---|---|---|---|
| Undercover parking (number of spaces) | | | |
| Hardstand for boat/caravan (Y/N) | | | |
| Level of finishes (good/average, etc.) | | | |
| Views (Y/N) | | | |
| Availability (Y/N) | | | |
| Other | | | |
| **Financial summary** | | | |
| Freehold (Y/N) | | | |
| Leasehold (Y/N) | | | |
| Loan/lease (Y/N) | | | |
| Loan/licence (Y/N) | | | |
| Fee cap (%) | | | |
| Number of years | | | |
| Fee per annum (%) | | | |
| DMF on entry/exit | | | |
| Capital gain split with complex owner | | | |
| Structure flexibility (Y/N) | | | |
| Resale commission (Y/N) | | | |

# Appendix C: Research comparison worksheet

| | | | |
|---|---|---|---|
| Refurbishment charge | | | |
| Resale guarantee (Y/N) | | | |
| General services (village) fee | | | |
| Contract costs (Y/N) | | | |
| Other fees | | | |
| **Preferred unit price range ($)** | | | |
| Studio apartment | | | |
| 1 bedroom apartment | | | |
| 2 bedroom apartment | | | |
| 1 bedroom villa | | | |
| 2 bedroom villa | | | |
| 2 bedroom + study villa | | | |
| 3 bedroom villa | | | |
| Deposit required | | | |
| Settlement period (days) | | | |
| Rates | | | |
| Body corporate fees | | | |

# Appendix D
# Moving house checklist

| Item | Target date | Completed |
|------|-------------|-----------|
| **Six weeks before moving** | | |
| Confirm the date of your move. | | |
| If you're renting, notify your landlord of your moving date. | | |
| Check your home insurance—make sure you have contents cover from the day you move in to your new home. | | |
| Obtain written quotes from several removal firms. Get references and check the limits of their insurance. | | |
| If you're not using professional removalists, organise a friends and family moving team. | | |
| Book a storage space unit if required. | | |
| Notify the electricity, gas and telephone companies of your departure. | | |
| Start getting rid of possessions you no longer need. Decide which items can be taken to a charity shop, sold at a car boot sale or offered to your family or friends. | | |

| | | |
|---|---|---|
| If you need new furniture or carpets, order them now and arrange delivery for when you move in. | | |
| **Four weeks before moving** | | |
| Have your car checked over, especially if you are going to be driving a long distance on moving day. | | |
| Notify Centrelink, the utility companies and your insurer of your new address. | | |
| Start packing up items from your shed and garage. | | |
| **Two weeks before moving** | | |
| Start packing non-essential items such as books and non-seasonal clothes into boxes. Mark each box for the room it belongs to in your new home. | | |
| Notify your doctor, dentist and optician if you're moving out of the area. | | |
| Notify your milkman and newspaper shop that you're moving and give them a date you want the service to stop. | | |
| If you have pets, arrange for someone to look after them during the move, or arrange their transportation. | | |
| Make a list of everyone who should know about the move. Send out change of address postcards. | | |

| | | |
|---|---|---|
| Finalise arrangements with your removal company. Confirm arrival times and make sure your removalists have directions to your new address. | | |
| Arrange a time to collect the keys for your new home. | | |
| **One week to go** | | |
| Contact internet provider and notify them of change of address. | | |
| Return any library books. | | |
| Make arrangements for your mail to be redirected to your new address. | | |
| Settle any outstanding bills for things like newspapers and milk deliveries. | | |
| Return any items you have borrowed from friends or neighbours. | | |
| **Three days to go** | | |
| Check that the keys to your new home are going to be available and make sure you arrange where to drop off your existing keys (to the estate agents or the new owners). | | |
| Organise a box or bag with essential items in it for the day of the move. | | |
| Inform neighbours about the removal van so that they can make alternative arrangements for parking if necessary. | | |
| **Two days to go** | | |
| Empty and defrost your fridge and freezer. | | |

| | | |
|---|---|---|
| Empty kitchen cupboards and throw out any food that you don't intend taking with you. | | |
| Collect any valuables and/or important documents together into one container which should travel with you and not in the removal van. | | |
| **One day to go** | | |
| Finish off any packing apart from the bathroom or kitchen where you'll still probably need to use essential items. | | |
| Dismantle any self-assembly furniture and disconnect the major electrical items such as the washing machine, computer, and hi-fi equipment. | | |
| Make up a snack box and a toiletries box for tomorrow. | | |
| Confirm arrival time with the removal company. | | |
| Charge your mobile phone as you will probably use it on moving day. | | |
| Finally, make sure you get a good night's sleep. You're going to be busy in the morning! | | |

# Appendix E
## Change of address checklist

| Organisation | Completed |
|---|---|
| Bank accounts | |
| Credit cards | |
| Store cards (for example, Flybuys, Myer card, David Jones card) | |
| Frequent flyer programs | |
| Internet service provider | |
| Telephone (land line) | |
| Mobile phone service provider | |
| Electricity | |
| Gas | |
| Council (rates) | |
| Post office (redirect mail) | |
| Insurance provider | |
| Wine club | |
| Financial adviser/accountant | |
| Solicitor | |
| Doctor | |
| Friends and family | |
| Workplace | |
| Library cards | |
| Book clubs | |

| | |
|---|---|
| Car registration | |
| Car insurance | |
| Car licence | |
| Centrelink | |
| Electoral roll | |
| Tax office | |
| Medicare | |
| Cable TV or broadband internet connection | |
| Other: | |
| | |
| | |
| | |
| | |

# Glossary

**accredited retirement village** Some retirement villages are accredited under the Retirement Village Association's national accreditation scheme, which sets benchmark standards for retirement villages.

**aged care** Aged care facilities offer enhanced care to individuals who can no longer live independently.

**assisted living unit** These small villa- or apartment-style properties provide residents with a higher level of care, services and assistance with day-to-day living activities.

**body corporate** Also known as the owners corporation, the body corporate is the committee of unit owners in strata-titled freehold properties that governs the complex within the limits of the body corporate charter and the relevant state community titles legislation.

**capital gain (growth)** The capital gain or growth of a unit is the amount by which the resale price exceeds the original purchase price.

**company title** Under a company title purchase arrangement, a corporation owns the village and a resident buys shares in the company at a price roughly equal to the freehold market value of the property. Share ownership confers the right to occupy the premises attached to those shares.

**Comparative Market Analysis (CMA)** A CMA is a free appraisal of value of a property by a real estate agent, rather than a professional, independent valuation.

**contract preparation costs** These costs are the expenses incurred by the village operator when preparing contracts for the purchase or resale of your unit.

**consumer price index (CPI)** Represented as a percentage, and used as a guide to assess movement in the cost of living, the CPI traces the relative changes in the cost of goods and services to a typical consumer over time.

**contract conveyancing** In the context of this book, contract conveyancing is the process of having a solicitor review your purchase contract.

**cooling-off period** Most state retirement villages legislation includes a provision for a cooling-off or settling-in period, during which a buyer can terminate the purchase contract.

**disclosure document** Also known as a public information document (PID), this document outlines key facts about a retirement village. Village operators in most states are required by law to provide it to a potential buyer before a contract is signed.

**deferred management fee (DMF)** Under DMF purchase arrangements, residents accrue a fee for each year of their occupation. The fee may be based on the original ingoing contribution or purchase price, or on the resale price of the unit, and is payable to the operator at exit.

**due diligence** A person performs due diligence by carefully researching all aspects and evaluating all potential risks of a purchase.

**exit entitlement** Under a DMF contract, this is the residual amount paid back to the resident after the unit has been sold and all management fees, commissions and costs have been subtracted.

**exit fee** Also known as a DMF or departure fee, this fee is encountered in loan/lease or loan/licence contracts as well as some freehold and leasehold contracts.

**freehold contract** In a freehold contract the title to the property is owned by the resident. Freehold retirement units are found in strata-titled communities and are similar to any freehold property based on a community title scheme, such as a block of units.

**general services charge** Also known as the village fee, this charge is levied against residents on a weekly, fortnightly or monthly basis to cover the operational expenses of the village, such as maintenance, power, insurance and management.

**independent living unit (ILU)** An ILU is an apartment, villa or townhouse designed for residents who do not require assistance with daily living activities.

**ingoing contribution** Unique to DMF contracts, and another name for the purchase price, this one-off fee is the amount payable under the contract to secure the right to reside in the retirement village.

**integrated care facility** These villages provide a range of different care levels within the same location. For example, they may offer residents independent living in units, villas or apartments, assisted living in serviced apartments and higher care hospital accommodation.

**leasehold contract** Under this purchase arrangement the resident owns the unit and leases the plot of land it sits on from the village operator. The resident pays an ongoing body corporate or owners corporation fee that covers the lease payment, rates and maintenance costs.

**loan/lease or loan/licence contract** Also known as a DMF contract, its main feature is the annual fee incurred by the resident for each year of occupancy up to a set number of years, calculated as a percentage of either the original purchase price or the resale value of the unit.

**not-for-profit organisation** The Australian Taxation Office accepts an organisation as not-for-profit if its constitution or governing documents prohibit distribution of profits or gains to individual members and its actions are consistent with this prohibition.

**occupation right** The right to occupy is the right of residents to occupy their unit under a lease or licence.

**owners corporation committee** Also known as a body corporate committee, and characteristic of strata-titled freehold villages, it is an elected representative committee of members, which governs the complex according to the owners corporation charter and the relevant state community titles legislation.

**penetration** In the retirement industry, penetration represents the proportion of a population aged over 65 years (the assumed age for entry into a retirement village) that actually lives in a retirement village.

**public information document (PID)** Also known as a disclosure document, the PID outlines key facts about a retirement village. In most states village operators are required by law to provide this document to potential purchasers before they sign a contract to purchase a property.

**registered retirement village** A retirement village can be registered under the retirement villages legislation and formally recognised by the administering office of the state government.

**rental model** Rental retirement villages, operating under state residential tenancies legislation, simply charge a weekly rent to the occupant on behalf of the unit owner, who may be an investor or a corporation.

**residents' committee** This formal, representative body of residents presents the views of residents to the village operator.

**resident–funded village** A strata–titled freehold village is governed by an owners corporation or body corporate committee. Under this model, administration, maintenance and running expenses are funded from a levy paid by residents.

**retirement living sector** The focus of the retirement living sector (as distinct from the aged care sector) is the provision of independent living accommodation for seniors, which may include a component of higher care provision.

**retirement village** As defined by the retirement villages legislation in each state, a retirement village is a residential complex predominantly occupied by retired people aged over 55.

**sales commission** This fee is the commission, paid by the seller to the selling agent, that is incurred with the successful sale of a unit or occupation right.

**serviced apartment** Typically smaller than independent living units, serviced apartments offer an enhanced level of care. The resident will pay a higher general services fee and receive services such as cleaning, meals and laundry.

**supported living facility** This model offers a blended aged care and retirement village facility, where residents live in their own apartments and any care services required—from cleaning and laundry through to palliative care—are brought to them in their home.

**turnover** In the retirement industry, turnover refers to the event of a resident leaving a retirement home (for whatever reason) and the resale of the unit to the next occupant.

**village operator** Most retirement villages are owner operated. However, in some villages the owner will employ an external company that specialises in managing retirement villages.

**village owner** In Australia, retirement village owners include corporations, church groups and charitable organisations, as well as family companies.

**waiting list** Operators of popular retirement villages often maintain a waiting list of prospective residents. There may or may not be a fee charged for placement on the list.

# Index

Printed in Australia
29 Sep 2017
648285

9 780730 377702